WATER FOR SALE

WATER FOR SALE

HOW BUSINESS AND THE MARKET CAN RESOLVE THE WORLD'S WATER CRISIS

FREDRIK SEGERFELDT

CATO INSTITUTE
WASHINGTON, D.C.

Originally published as *Vatten till salu. Hur företag och marknad kan lösa världens vattenkris,* copyright ©2003 Timbro, Stockholm.

This English-language edition has been revised.

Library of Congress Cataloging-in-Publication Data

Segerfeldt, Fredrik.
    [Vatten till salu. English]
    Water for sale : how businesses and the market can resolve the world's water crisis / Fredrik Segerfeldt.
       p. cm.
    Rev. translation of: Vatten till salu.
    Includes bibliographical references and index.
    ISBN 1-930865-76-7 (alk. paper)
    1. Water resources development—Developing countries.
    2. Water-supply—Developing countries.   I. Title.

HD1702.S4413 2005
333.91′009172′4—dc22

                          2005047027

Cover design by Jon Meyers.
Printed in the United States of America.

CATO INSTITUTE
1000 Massachusetts Ave., N.W.
Washington, D.C. 20001

"Centuries of experience show that governments are more capable of regulating the behavior of private sector interests than they are of increasing the efficiency of bureaucrats."
Christopher Lingle, *Korea Times*, June 14, 2001

"All the water there will be, is."
Anonymous

"Thousands have lived without love, not one without water."
W. H. Auden

Contents

Contents

Preface

When I told friends and colleagues I was writing a book about water, and the role of markets and the private sector in water distribution in developing countries, most of them frowned and asked why. True, at first this seems to be a very technical and narrow subject. But on closer inspection, one comes to realize that there is a global drama taking place. It is not primarily about water technology; it is about more than a billion people around the world lacking access to clean and safe water, which causes 12 million deaths a year. Therefore, this became more a mission of life and death than yet another boring technical study. It is my hope that readers will find the book as important as I think the topic is.

Preface

Acknowledgments

I was first asked to write this book by Fredrik Erixon, chief economist at Timbro, the Swedish think tank. I had no idea when accepting the project that I was about to dive deep down into the blue. Fredrik provided me with excellent coaching throughout the project, for which I am grateful. I would also like to thank friends and colleagues for reading and commenting on the drafts.

It is not possible to list all the publications I have drawn upon for this book, but the works of Roger Bate have been important as a source of inspiration. He is extensively quoted here. Thanks also to Linda Bergman and Jorge Dell'Oro, who organized an excellent program for me in Buenos Aires.

The topic of this book is a very important one, and I am therefore very pleased that the book is being published in English. For this I am indebted to the Cato Institute and its director of the Project on Global Economic Liberty, Ian Vásquez. I also thank Roger Tanner, who translated the text from Swedish, and Lisa Wolff, who copyedited the American edition.

CHAPTER ONE

Introduction

Milagros Quirino and Fely Griarte live in a poor part of the Philippine capital, Manila. For most of their lives, lack of clean and safe water was a major problem. They had to do with only a few liters of water a day. Usually they bought it from a neighbor family that owns a deep-water well. About 3,000 families in the neighborhood used to share three such wells. "We often had to get up at 3 A.M. to make sure we would get water," said Fely. "And if there was a power cut and the water pump did not work, we would have to wait another day." The quality of the water was poor, and it had to be boiled before use.[1]

The situation Milagros and Fely experienced, and worse, is shared by many. Throughout the world, 1.1 billion people do not have access to clean and safe water. This figure has held constant for decades. Most of them live in poor countries. The shortage of water has fearful consequences in the form of poverty, disease, and death. Ninety-seven percent of all water distribution in poor countries is managed by public suppliers, who are responsible for more than a billion people being without water. To overcome this problem, some governments of impoverished nations have turned to business enterprise for help, usually with good results.

In poor countries with private investments in the water sector, more people have access to water than in those without such investments. Moreover, there are many good examples of business enterprise successfully improving water distribution there. Millions of people who previously lacked water mains within reach are now getting clean and safe water delivered within a convenient distance and are spared all the privations that water shortage entails.

Milagros and Fely are among these lucky few, since they happen to live in a city where reforms have been undertaken. Two private companies have taken over the water distribution and have reached millions of residents who previously were not served by the public utility. During that time, connections to the water supply systems were not possible because the families have no land titles. The residents, therefore, were delighted when staff from one of the water companies, Manila Water, in a special project targeting poor neighborhoods, came to their area in 2000 to introduce the project, in which residents no longer need land titles to be served by the company. They now not only have access to clean water 24 hours a day, but the water is cheaper. While they used to pay 100 pesos for 1 cubic meter, the cost is now only 15 pesos, including 7 pesos set aside for operation and maintenance. Milagros and Fely, together with millions of other Manila residents, are much better off.

But the "privatization" of water distribution has stirred up strong feelings and has met with resistance in various parts of the world. Googling for "water privatization" on the Internet yields 1,750,000 hits, many concerning various kinds of opposition to the involvement of commercial interests in water supply. And indeed there have been violent protests and demonstrations against water privatization all over the world, not least at the G8 meeting of June 2003, which, ironically, was held in the French town of Evian, famed for its mineral water.

The water supply issue has been the subject of a succession of activities at the supreme level of international politics. The United

Nations has discussed it, and several UN agencies are very actively addressing water supply in poor countries. One of the organization's Millennium Development Goals is to halve the number of people in the world without access to safe drinking water. Three World Water Forums have been devoted to world water supply. These meetings have been surrounded by protests and demonstrations, and some of them have been virtually sabotaged by hard-line opponents of privatization. There is feverish international activity concerning the world's water supplies, above all in poor countries, and a very fierce debate is in progress concerning the role of business enterprise and the market in this context.

Opponents of privatization look askance at the possibility of making money from people's need for water and fear that the poor will have this fundamental necessity taken away from them if they cannot pay for it. Water, they argue, is a human right that the public sector is duty-bound to provide to the population. Claude Généreux, vice president of the Canadian Union of Public Employees, has put the argument simply: "Water is a basic human right, not a commodity to be bought, sold and traded."[2] Other opponents use slogans like "People do not drink money, we drink water" and "No profits from water."[3]

Simplistic arguments like this do not present any alternative solution and are founded on ideological conviction, not facts.

Many of the active protagonists in this debate are the selfsame nongovernmental organizations (NGOs) and individuals within the anti-globalization movement who used to campaign for restrictions on international trade. Having lost the debate on free trade, they are now looking for new adversaries and new expressions of international enterprise to attack. Public-sector employee unions and other organizations with a powerful vested interest in water remaining under public auspices constitute another group. A third group is the media, which have given the issue generous but slanted coverage. These three groups are found above all in affluent countries. Activist organizations in developing countries make up a fourth group, albeit more limited. Let us take a closer look at these different groups, as an introduction.

Given the capital failure of the public sector to supply poor people with clean water, the positions and actions of anti-privatization activists are hard to understand. In light of the overwhelming evidence, one cannot help drawing the conclusion that they are driven by an ideologically inspired aversion to enterprise, coupled with fear on the part of vested interests of losing their privileges. These groups share a belief in the superior ability of the public sector to deliver what citizens want, along with a profound suspicion of the market economy and business enterprise in general and Western big business in particular.

The American Corpwatch organization claims that business interests are waging an aggressive campaign for control of the world's water. Public Citizen, under the witty headline "Resist the corporation tidal wave," maintains that "the multinationals try to keep the global water agenda in their hands in order to privatize every aspect of our global commons." A union activist maintains, "Money should be spent on developing water infrastructure in the poor townships—not lining the pockets of the water multinationals."[4] This is the kind of argumentation and rhetoric on which the debate is being centered.

But there are players who address the problem in a purely pragmatic light. South Africa's Water Affairs and Forestry Minister from 1999 to 2004, Ronald Kasrils, is a former Marxist who has taken a very open-minded position on the involvement of business in water distribution. He argues that, with so many South Africans still without water, and given the huge resources needed in order to reach them all, turning to the private sector for help is very often a matter of necessity:

The involvement of the private sector in delivery of services to the people of South Africa is not a question of principle, but one of practice.[5]

This statement comes in stark contrast to the dogmatism of the previously mentioned opponents. Unlike them, Kasrils puts water supply before ideology.

But the protests and demonstrations have left their mark. Privatization has decelerated, and the World Bank, which used to be one of the prime movers for admitting enterprise, has gone on the defensive, so the danger is that the improvements achieved by giving more scope to the market and enterprise will grind to a halt or even come to nothing. International water companies are also having second thoughts, bowing to popular pressure from many directions. As David Boys, from Public Service International, an international labor union representing public employees, and one of the most fervent anti-privatization campaigners, puts it:

There is evidence that water corporations are already backing out of the developing world because of tough civil pressure.[6]

It is vital, then, for the issue of water privatization in poor countries to be discussed on the basis of facts and serious analysis, instead of being reduced to a matter of dogmas, simplifications, and half-truths—not least in order for those who at present are without water to be given access to it. For there are many good arguments in favor of allowing business enterprise and the market more scope in the water supply of poor countries. And so it would be not just a pity but quite outrageous if millions of people were to starve, fall ill, and die through water shortages brought about by the strident propaganda of vested interests and powerfully ideological movements with quite different ends in view.

Many people instinctively think it must be wrong to claim that Western multinationals are better at supplying water for the poor. Even people who normally have pro-market preferences tend to argue along the lines that it is dangerous to rely on profit-seeking enterprises for the provision of this vital good. One of the ambitions of this book is to show that you do not have to be a hard-core libertarian to believe in the importance of letting the market and the private sector play a bigger role in the water provision of developing countries. You just have to be pragmatic and look at what works and what does not. The evidence is as clear as it can be.

In this book, then, we will be leaving dogmatism and ideology aside in order to discuss why water distribution in poor countries is in such a wretched state, what has been done, and what can be done.

CHAPTER TWO

Aqua Vitae

Water is vital. Our bodies are about 60 to 70 percent water, and we normally need a daily intake of about 3 or 4 liters. People feel thirsty after losing only 1 percent of their fluid, and when the loss approaches 10 percent their lives are in danger. We can survive for only a few days without water. But water is also used for other things besides regulating the fluid balance of the human body; it is used for everything from cooking and washing to irrigation and industrial activity. Water is necessary to survival, and it is the basis of all life.

This is what makes it so serious that the world's water supply is in crisis. Things are the worst in the big cities of the Third World. In Bandung, Indonesia, for example, 62 percent of the population are not served by the main water network, in common with the same percentage of the population of Maputo, Mozambique, and 50 percent of the people in Madras, India.[7]

The sewerage situation is even worse. Some 2.4 billion people — more than a third of the earth's population — do not have access to effective sanitation. Lack of water and sewerage has fearful consequences for human life.

Every year, more than a billion people contract water-related diseases. At any given time, close to half of the urban population in Africa, Asia, and Latin America are suffering from one or more of the main diseases associated with inadequate water and sanitation provision. Three out of every four cases of illness in Bangladesh are connected with foul water and poor sanitary conditions. Water shortage accounts for 12 million deaths annually. In other words, every minute of every day, 22 people die because they cannot get enough safe water. In 2003, probably more people suffered and died from lack of safe water than as a result of armed conflicts.[8]

As usual, it is the children who suffer most. Every year, 3 million children die from water-borne diseases such as cholera and other diarrheal disorders. As often as every 10 seconds, a child dies from a water-borne disease that could have been prevented.[9]

Access to safe water and effective sanitation can save many lives. A review of several studies has shown the number of water-related deaths in groups gaining access to safe water and effective sanitation to have declined on average by no less than 69 percent. One study shows that infant and child mortality declined in the same way by no less than 55 percent. Another study estimates that the potential reduction in mortality for 18 diseases as a result of improvements in water supply and sanitation range from 40 to 100 percent. Health-related problems caused by lack of water and sanitation are particularly striking in cities. In the urban areas of low-income countries, one child in six dies before the age of five. In areas with a bad supply of water and poor sanitation, the child mortality rate is multiplied by 10 or 20 compared to areas with adequate water and sanitation services.[10]

Health problems do not only cause human suffering. They can also be very costly for a country as a whole. A cholera epidemic (caused by inadequate water supply and sanitation) in Peru in 1991 is estimated to have caused a net economic loss of $495 million, more than twice as much money as it would take to provide all unserved Peruvians with standpost water.[11]

This takes us straight to the economic aspects of water shortage, such as hunger and poverty. There are roughly as many extremely poor people in the world (people living on less than a dollar a day) as there are people without access to safe water. In fact, these are to a great extent the same people. What they need is economic growth. Yet the lack of access to water hampers growth.

The world's worst poverty is in part due to substandard food production. Since access to, and proper use of, water is essential to greater agricultural efficiency, water shortage is one factor that leads to poverty. The UN finds that "there is a strong positive link between investment in irrigation, poverty alleviation and food security."[12]

Good health is another factor that facilitates growth, and access to safe water is the be-all and end-all when it comes to improving the health status of poor countries. Ill health and poverty are also closely interlinked, in the sense that illness becomes expensive in poor countries. In Karachi, Pakistan, for example, poor people who live in districts with no sewerage and who have had no training in hygiene spend six times as much on medical care as people in districts with sewerage who have a basic knowledge of domestic hygiene.[13]

A third, often neglected, link between water and poverty is the fact that many people in poor countries spend a lot of time—as much as six hours a day in some cases—fetching water. Often they have to walk several miles carrying heavy vessels of water. Most often this work is done by women and children. Women and girls the world over are estimated to spend 10 million person-years, annually, fetching water.[14] This makes it impossible for them to attend school, do homework, or have a job. In this way water shortage traps them in poverty, and the world as a whole suffers a tremendous economic loss.

There is also a connection between water and industrial development. Industry is often dependent on water in large quantities, and a supply of good-quality water, reasonably priced, is a *sine qua non* of industrial development. Good water quality is often a criterion for the localization of growth-promoting investments. Let me cite an example. According to one estimate, Nakuru, the third-largest city in Kenya, has lost many investments and, consequently, job opportunities because of its poor water supply, at the same time that the Kenyan government is devoting no less than 13 percent of public spending to water projects.[15]

Pure Water and Growth in Macao, China

In 1985 the Macao authorities signed a concession contract with a private company. The quantity and quality of water greatly improved. Ten years later the city's gross domestic product had tripled. Macao today has one of the highest living standards anywhere in Asia. Even though the improvement in water distribution is not the main reason for the economic miracle, it is unlikely that such impressive development would have been possible without it.

Source: Asian Development Bank (2000).

Most experts agree that mankind's water shortage is going to increase unless something is done about it. The earth's population will increase by 2 billion over the next 30 years and by a further billion during the 20 years thereafter. Most of these people will live in cities in developing countries.[16] The UN expects 2.7 billion people to be experiencing a severe water shortage in 2025. That is no less than a third of the earth's population. During this period it is feared that 76 million people will die from water-related diseases that are preventable.

This growing population will also require additional food production. Ninety percent of that increase will have to be achieved on existing arable land. Food productivity, in other words, will have to be doubled, which in turn will require more water.[17]

Finally, lack of water, just as shortages of many other scarce resources, is a source of conflicts between countries and provinces as well as between interest groups and individuals. Since water is so important for life, health, and development, these conflicts sometimes take a violent form.

Water shortage is nothing new. Just as hunger was a common state among primitive peoples, so thirst and water supply have been a problem for many for the greater part of human history. It is unacceptable, though, that in the 21st century, with prosperity multiplied several times over, poverty reduced, and technical progress accelerating all the time, billions of people still have difficulty obtaining clean water.

Why, then, are so many people bereft of water and sewerage? Opinions vary on this point. In the UN Millennium Declaration, the heads of state and government of the international community set themselves the target of halving, by 2015, the proportion of people without sustainable access to safe drinking water. This goal was reaffirmed in 2002 at the Johannesburg World Summit on Sustainable Development, which added the goal of halving by 2015 the proportion of people without access to basic sanitation. Both summits, however, were vague as to how this should be accomplished, which in turn reflects the prevalent disunity on the issue.[18]

There are those who take the shortage of *access* to safe water to mean a shortage of *water as such*. There simply isn't enough water to supply the world's growing population, the argument goes, and so we must find better ways of saving water in the affluent world and perhaps even share it with others.

It is true that the earth's population has multiplied very swiftly. But is the quantity of water really the main problem? To investigate this we will now turn to considering how much water there is in the world, what the situation looks like in different countries with different amounts of water and different levels of development, and to what extent the shortage of water can be attributed to economic and political causes.

CHAPTER THREE

Shortage of Good Policies, Not of Water

Of course, the supply of water is not unlimited. The earth holds only a certain amount. Water is a finite resource. In principle, though, the supply of water is so great as to be infinite for all human purposes. No less than two-thirds of the earth's surface is water. True, the greater part is salt water or else water trapped in ice. But that still leaves 13,500 km³, or 2,300,000 liters per capita.[19]

Every year, 113,000 km³ of water falls to the earth. Of this, 72,000 km³ evaporates, leaving a net precipitation of 41,000 km³. That equals roughly 19,000 liters per person daily, a quite fantastic figure. Consumption today is about 1,300 liters per person daily, that is, only 6.8 percent of what it could be.[20]

The UN calculates somewhat differently, maintaining that every year we use 8 percent of the water that exists and pointing out that water is a renewable resource, that is, can be used over and over again.[21] Even though assessments diverge, they agree that what we are using is far from all the water available. The problem is not the amount of water available but the lack of development in poor countries.

There are many countries with quite copious precipitation where nevertheless only a few people have access to safe water. And there are countries with quite meager precipitation where everyone has access to safe water. In Cambodia, Rwanda, and Haiti, only 32, 41,

Figure 3.1. Supply of safe water in countries with different levels of development.

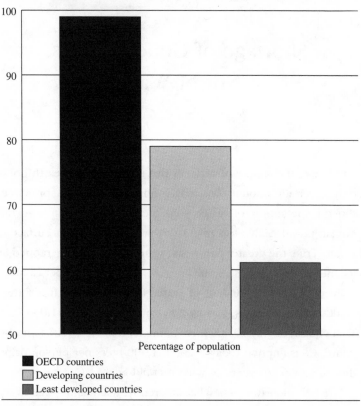

Percentage of population

■ OECD countries
▢ Developing countries
■ Least developed countries

Source: World Development Indicators, WDI online.

and 46 percent of the population respectively have access to safe water. These countries have more annual rainfall than Australia, and yet 100 percent of Australia's inhabitants have access to safe water. Cherrapunji in India, although officially the wettest place on earth, has recurrent water shortages.[22] It is the level of development that determines access to water, not the amount of rainfall.

Looking at the countries that are short of water and comparing this with their level of development, one can clearly see that there is a very strong link between shortage of water and shortage of development. (See figure 3.1.)

An average of 99 percent of the population in the Organization for Economic Cooperation and Development countries have access to safe water. In developing countries the corresponding figure is 79 percent, and in the least developed countries it is only 61 percent.[23] The connection is obvious. However, the category *developing country* includes countries at very different stages of development, and among them, the correlation between income level and adequate water supply is not so strong. Rather, there is actually an astonishing level of difference between countries at similar levels of development, suggesting that policies matter a lot, as we shall see later.[24]

Once again, then, the problem is not the amount of water available but the inability to produce and distribute safe water.[25] A distinction can therefore be drawn between *physical* and *economic* water shortage. *Physical* water shortage is mainly confined to countries of the Arab world, a number of places in South and East Asia, and parts of Australia. Another source projects that in 2025 there will be *physical* water scarcity only in the extreme south of Africa, in parts of South and East Asia, and to some extent in the Arab world. But there will be *economic* water scarcity in much of the global south.[26]

In China and India, for example, water is plentiful, but only 16 and 18 percent, respectively, of the water available to households, agriculture, and industry is used.[27] Kenya has the potential for supplying its entire population with water, but its water resources are underexploited. Kenya could produce upwards of 20 billion m^3 per annum, which is far in excess of the 3.56 billion m^3 it is expected to need in 2010.[28]

There are those who claim that the connection between development and water shortage is the reverse, meaning that development creates water shortage, or that development makes us consume more and more water, which in the long run would be untenable.

This need not, however, be the case. Water use in the United States stopped rising in 1980, yet the nation's gross domestic product has grown steadily since then.[29] Economic growth need not mean using more resources, but it can mean using resources more efficiently. In 1930, for example, it took 200 metric tons of water to make a metric ton of steel. Today it takes only 20 metric tons of water, and the most efficient Korean manufacturers use only 3 or 4 metric tons.[30]

Lack of development, then, accounts for a good deal of the water shortage. But development is too complex and long-term a phenomenon to be the solution to this acute crisis. Too many people are dying too fast for us to wait for all countries to attain the degree of development today characterizing the OECD countries (the level at which everyone has access to safe water). Development alone will not solve the water shortage of poor countries. A faster and better solution is better governance, as has been observed in a number and variety of contexts. In the preliminary conclusions from the third World Water Forum we read:

> Many countries face a *governance* crisis, rather than a water crisis [emphasis added].[31]

The UN speaks in similar terms:

> The crisis is one of water governance, essentially caused by the ways in which we mismanage water.[32]

A Canadian research institute expresses it thus:

> The continuing mismanagement of the world's supply of fresh water poses the greatest threat to its availability and quality. That threat will grow as demand increases, particularly in developing countries.[33]

There is incomplete agreement, however, as to the nature of the political problems.

The role of the public sector has been under debate for several decades. During this time the sector itself has expanded heavily, not least in the affluent world. The average fiscal pressure (i.e., total tax receipts as a percentage of GDP), both in the OECD countries and in the European Union, is much heavier today than it was 30 years ago. But at the same time many countries have opened up their public sectors to competition and private initiatives. In Sweden, as in many other countries, we now have private television and radio channels, private hospitals, day nurseries, and schools run under private auspices and electricity companies listed on the stock exchange.

The great majority of people are very much in favor of this. Even politicians and debaters with their hearts on the left have assimilated the benefits of business enterprise in terms of competition, entrepreneurship, innovations, efficiency improvements, and better goods and services delivered to customers and citizens.

But on the particular subject of water there seems to be a special degree of resistance. So in this publication I set out to show that there are good reasons for allowing the market and business more scope in matters of water supply because there are strong arguments to suggest that the real trouble with present-day water policy is public-sector control of distribution in poor countries.

Why, UN-Habitat asks, are so many people left without adequate water and sanitation "after 50 years of aid programs, dozens of official aid agencies and development banks and hundreds of international NGOs with programs for water and sanitation?"[34]

Simplifying somewhat, there are three different water policy problems in developing countries. The first is connected with investments in water distribution, as regards both quantity and quality. The second is a number of weaknesses generally present in public activity and especially in water distribution in poor countries. We shall be discussing these two problems in the present chapter. The third problem concerns the laws and regulations applying to water, such as inadequate or nonexistent property rights and inappropriate pricing. These demand to be discussed at greater length and will therefore be dealt with in separate chapters. Two more chapters will then address, respectively, the possibilities and risks that privatization entails, and we shall be considering a number of instances where the private sector has been given a role in water distribution. First, though, let us consider investment problems.

Investments Are Inadequate, in Terms of Both Quantity and Quality

Much of the shortage of safe water and sanitation in the Third World can be attributed to underinvestment and lack of maintenance. Quite simply, the infrastructure needed for supplying people with water has not been built. This involves everything from the collection of water to its purification and distribution. The public sector has failed to lay down mains for households or communities. Meanwhile, the infrastructure that does exist has not been properly maintained. The pipes leak, and the water is either dirty when put into the system or else gets sullied by the pipes. This deficiency is partly due to a failure of political priorities. Investments in fresh water have long been neglected in poor countries. Less than 5 percent of infrastructure investments in the developing countries have concerned the water sector. In many poor countries, the water-supply investment stock is only 1 percent of the figure for industrialized nations with similar climatic conditions. [36] But of course, these underinvestments are also a consequence of developing countries being just that—developing countries. They are poor, and capital is in shorter supply than in rich countries. Quite simply, neither the public sector nor local private-sector firms have enough money to finance the investments needed.

In a report compiled by the World Water Council, an international think-tank whose membership includes international organizations, governments, NGOs, and the private sector, it was estimated that over the next 25 years as much as $180 billion per annum would have to be invested, mostly in developing and transitional countries, to guarantee universal access to safe water and sanitation. This amount has been questioned by some, but according to the World Panel on Financing Water Infrastructure, the so-called Camdessus report, this figure is "generally accepted as the right order of magnitude."[36] It is a huge amount of money, which many developing countries will have great difficulty in raising. Investments today are running at $70 or $80 billion per annum—less than half of what will be needed.[37] Most observers agree that neither the developing countries themselves nor development assistance will be able to meet this requirement. By way of comparison, total public development assistance in 2003—that is, not just for water supply but for all purposes—amounted to some $69 billion, a little more than a third of the investment needed. So even if public development assistance worldwide were to double and focus exclusively on building up viable water distribution systems in developing countries, this would still not be enough. The Camdessus report also highlighted the fact that meeting the UN Millennium Goal of halving the number of people without water and sanitation by 2015 means a daily connection rate of several hundred thousand people.

Underinvestments and lack of maintenance have resulted in many people being excluded from water and sewerage networks, in water pipes leaking, in no meters existing so that payment can be collected, and in the water supplied being of inferior quality and sporadically available. There are many Southeast Asian cities where water is piped to households for only a couple of hours per day, and even then not every day. These countries simply cannot afford to supply their citizens with safe water.

But the quantity of investments is not the only problem. Their quality is a problem of at least the same magnitude. Third World public water investments are often characterized by huge dam projects, financed as a rule with a combination of development aid and national government revenue. Usually these projects are poorly designed, shoddily built, and badly managed, so the outcome is far worse than anticipated. In addition they often cost the taxpayers a great deal of money and preempt resources that could have been more usefully applied to other purposes.

William Finnegan of the *New Yorker* accurately describes the World Bank's past lending for water development in poor countries:

> The Bank once had a quite different approach to public works: it was an enthusiastic financier of monumental projects, and would typically lend the money to build large dams. Many of the dams were spectacular failures, delivering few, if any, benefits (except to politicians and construction firms).[38]

Bad Public-Sector Investments in Peru and Sri Lanka

By the end of 1993 the government of Peru had spent $3.4 billion on nine different large-scale water projects. Although several of the projects had been completed decades earlier, they had achieved only 6.6 percent of the anticipated outcome in terms of creating new land for farming (through irrigation with water from dams), and not one single kilowatt-hour of electricity had been generated. The cost of the irrigated farmland created came to between $10,000 and $56,000 per hectare, whereas normal irrigable land in the same region costs $3,000. Millions of dollars had thus been squandered on grandiose but ineffective showcase projects.

In Sri Lanka the Mahaweli Development Program, at worst, took as much as 44 percent of all public investment, no less than 6 percent of GDP. This can be compared with the 20 or 25 percent of public infrastructure investments that water resources development most often accounts for in Asian countries. The cost of the project rose so high as to make the new farmland hugely expensive, forcing the government to subsidize the land. This in turn created severe social tensions, because the money for the subsidies had to be taken from other items of expenditure, and because those allotted land were considered to have obtained unfair advantages.

Source: Holden and Thobani (1996).

Government spending on water infrastructure has often had seriously adverse effects on the environment as well. Widespread public interference in Pakistan has resulted in nearly 10 percent of the cultivable land suffering from salination. When the groundwater of coastal regions is overexploited, saltwater penetrates the water table, making both water and cultivable land unserviceable. This has happened, for example, in Saudi Arabia, Bahrain, Gujarat (India), and Java.

The best-known, and environmentally most horrific, public water infrastructure project was undertaken in the Soviet Union during the 1950s, when, in order to provide water for cotton plantations, the Soviet authorities diverted the two largest rivers of Central Asia, which watered the Aral Sea. The result was an immense ecological disaster. The lake was diminished by 66 percent and its salinity rose drastically. Salt and pesticides from the dried-out lake bed were picked up by the wind, the storms that followed made the land for miles around the lake impossible to farm, any number of people developed health problems, and the fish died out.

Weaknesses of Water Bureaucracies

This discussion of large-scale public-sector initiatives brings us directly to one of the principal points, namely the workings of water bureaucracies in poor countries. These tend to display weaknesses in everything from lack of competence and administrative acumen to political control and perverse incentive structures.

Fragmented Water Bureaucracy in Ethiopia

Up until the beginning of the 1990s, eight different authorities were involved in Ethiopia's water management, resulting in much unnecessary duplication and in heavy wastage of resources on a myriad of independent and semi-autonomous authorities and organizations. Added to which large parts of the country were left out of the water and sewerage network.

On top of this, water policy is excessively centralized, both politically and administratively. Centralization paves the way for political control, lends added weight to bureaucracy, and removes investment decisionmaking a long way away from the on-the-ground reality. The players with decisionmaking powers are too far away from the places where the consequences of their decisions are noticeable, and the people affected are too far away from the center of power to have any say in matters. SIDA (the Swedish International Development Cooperation Agency) notes:

> There are many examples of failed facilities and inappropriate solutions imposed on communities by central authorities. . . . Development based on bottom-up demand for services by consumers who are aware of feasible choices and their associated costs are believed far more appropriate in the future.[39]

It may seem contradictory to argue that a phenomenon is at one and the same time fragmented and overcentralized, but it is not. There is no contradiction between deficient bureaucratic coordination—that is to say, horizontal fragmentation between different authorities and agencies—and an excessive degree of vertical centralization between central power and local and regional authorities.

Public water distribution, moreover, most often has limited access to, or knowledge of, the latest technology, and its in-house water management expertise is often minimal. As a result, authorities are unable to collect or use the water available and unable to distribute water to the population as efficiently as possible. One survey showed that in 32 out of 50 Asian cities, water spillage exceeded 30 percent. Spillage in Latin America accounts for 40 to 70 percent of the water produced under public auspices. Other sources indicate that water spillage in developing countries averages no less than 40 percent of all water produced. In Bangladesh, the Philippines, and Thailand, as much as 50 percent of water is wasted.[40]

In order to charge money for water, one must be able to measure how much of it consumers use. But in most developing countries with public water supplies, metering works badly. A survey of 50 Asian cities revealed that public water distributors measured consumption for only half the users.[41]

But this lack of water consumption metering in public water régimes does not only illustrate weaknesses in terms of competence and technology. It also clearly reveals the workings of a public authority and the incentives it faces. A private firm, whose livelihood depends on earnings exceeding expenditure, is very strongly motivated to measure its customers' consumption; otherwise, the firm will not know how much to charge. Without income it cannot invest in new infrastructure, or maintain the existing infrastructure, in which case it will enter a vicious circle of progressively fewer people having access to progressively deteriorating water.

Similarly, a public authority lacks incentives for reaching as many users as possible. A company operating on a commercial basis earns money for each new customer and therefore wants to reach as many users as possible. Bureaucracies, by contrast, depend for their survival not on earnings, but on funding allocations. Just like other public-sector operations, they are governed by a predetermined budget. If they do not spend all the money allocated to them, they usually get less money the following year. They therefore have no incentive to cut costs and run a surplus. (Some bureaucracies also measure their own performance by money spent, rather than by the result achieved.) By the same token, bureaucracies that spend all the money allocated to them tend to ask for a larger share of public funds, instead of finding ways of becoming more efficient. They are not rewarded if they do a good job. The budget mentality of bureaucracies therefore results in their having higher cost structures than private firms, which are constantly having to curb expenditure in order to post a profit.

Then there is the difference in degrees of innovation and renewal. A private firm competing with other firms for the customers' favor must always be devising new and better methods and must be as efficient as possible. This applies both at the procurement stage, in order to win the contract, and during the distribution process, to ensure that earnings exceed expenditure.

Distorted incentive structures exist not only at system level but also among individual officials in water bureaucracies. A public servant is very seldom rewarded for zeal in repairing ruptured pipes or laying new ones in new areas. Nor are water price rises very popular. On the other hand, big projects catching the attention of media and the general public often bring both recognition and power.

Another weakness lies in the inability of public bureaucracies as a rule to anticipate needs and demand. They cannot take in the myriad of signals about prices, demand, and changes in customers' habits and preferences the way private players operating in a market can. Even though the need for water is more stable than consumption of other goods, water distribution is often impeded by the inflexibility and organizational inertia of the administration. On top of this, public operations are often less expert in modern operational management. These weaknesses, in principle, do not distinguish poor countries from affluent ones, but the problem is greater in developing countries.

The politicization of water distribution and the corruption this entails are no less problematic. When politicians have complete control of where, when, and how water is to be produced and distributed, this entails any number of risks. First, major infrastructure projects are undertaken for political rather than economic reasons, in which case, more often than not, they go wrong. The Peruvian and Sri Lankan infrastructure projects presented in the previous box typify the negative effects of political control. The case of Cochabamba, Bolivia, reviewed later, is also a striking illustration of the negative effects of political interference and misjudgments in the construction of water infrastructure. Not infrequently, political prestige is principally to blame for such white elephants.

Another problem is that water is usually handled by state-owned enterprises that are used to channel assets to the politicians themselves and their supporters. Researchers have shown that corruption is common in large public water projects, and in the Third World the interests of water producers are often put before those of the urban poor. Corruption also occurs on a lesser scale, in the form of employees selling water on the side (e.g., by charging customers to turn a blind eye to illegal mains connections), tampering with users' bills, or allowing people to cut in line for mains water supply.

Politicians are above all anxious to please the constituents and groups on whom they depend for their reelection. Often these people are not the ones most in need of water, but advantaged groups like urban middle classes and well-organized big farmers. It can even happen that politicians deliberately retain systems that are economically inefficient but politically useful, because of the power that politicians and bureaucrats derive from them. This is the case, for example, when the price of water is kept down in order to raise demand. Politicians can then use quotas or other instruments to ensure that the water goes where it will do them, not the nation, the most good. Not surprisingly, quotas are also the most common way of regulating water demand in the least developed countries (LDCs). Landowners as a group often benefit greatly from low water prices, because when the price of water goes down, farmland prices go up. In this way, politicians can both butter up the big farmers and keep them to heel.

Moreover, politicians as a general rule are bad at deciding where water will confer the greatest economic benefit. There are innumerable examples of political control, even if well-intended, causing water to be used for activities that confer less than optimal benefit. For example, water is often steered, by means of quotas and subsidies, into agriculture, which is then able to produce more water-intensive crops than necessary, while industries that could make a bigger return on the same amount of water either have to go without or else have to pay more for it. André de Moor has estimated public subsidies to irrigation in developing countries to be between $20 and $25 billion annually.[42] Economic efficiency is then distorted, and the country as a whole is made poorer than it otherwise would be.

When discussing political control, it should also be remembered that a nation's political leaders are not always amicably disposed toward their population or intent on providing them the greatest possible benefit. They are not always dependent on meeting the needs of as many people as possible, and they have no intention of letting the people decide whether or not they are to stay in power. Private businesses, however, are bound by the contracts they have signed and also dependent on customers appreciating and being ready to pay for the goods or services delivered.

One aspect of water policy that is frequently overlooked is the lack of free trade in agricultural produce. This kind of trade could be thought of as trade in virtual water. Water is the most important input commodity for agricultural produce, so when buying produce from another country one is above all consuming that country's water. There are extensive trade barriers where agricultural produce is concerned, and many countries apply a policy of self-sufficiency in foodstuffs. As a result, many agricultural products are grown in places where conditions for growing them are less favorable than elsewhere, and so agriculture consumes an unnecessarily large amount of water. Freer trade in agricultural produce, then, would reduce water consumption worldwide.

It is primarily in the developing countries that people do not have access to clean, safe water. That is where the shortage of capital and competence is greatest. The public water régimes of the developing countries, quite simply, have failed to deliver clean, safe water, reasonably priced, to as many people as possible. The Asian Development Bank has shown that in Asian countries with a weak tax base—which is to say, most Asian countries except South Korea and Japan—efficient and dependable production and distribution of water is more the exception than the rule.[43] Often the water is not potable, is not available twenty-four hours a day, and is of very poor quality. In short, public water supply in poor countries usually has a low level of coverage, large quantities of spillage, minimal metering of consumption, and prices that are not proportional to costs. The victims, more often than not, are the very poorest inhabitants of the poor countries.

CHAPTER FOUR

Water Rights—The Solution to Many Problems

One big problem with the laws and regulations governing the world's water is the lack of property rights, especially the lack of rights to own water, and the lack of land titles in informal settlements in developing countries. This chapter deals primarily with the former, rights of water use, commonly referred to as *water rights*. This deficiency has negative consequences, which among other things include over-exploitation, economic losses, and conflicts. The problems of unregistered dwellers will be discussed only briefly toward the end of the chapter. Water-related conflicts will be discussed in Chapter 5.

"The tragedy of the commons," a popular theoretical concept in conservationist and environmentalist circles, was minted in 1968 by the American biologist Garreth Hardin in a classic article published by the journal *Science* and has come to stand for the environmental destruction that occurs when there are many individuals jointly using a scarce resource.[44] Hardin instanced this with shepherds using the same common as pasture for their flocks. As he saw it, any rational shepherd would graze as many of his animals there as possible, even though this spelled the destruction of the grazing land. This is because the benefit from being able to feed ne maximum number of animals accrues to the shepherd, while the cost of a common being destroyed has to be borne jointly by all shepherds and is thus exceeded by the gain to the individual shepherd.

Hardin showed that no one assumes responsibility for the common, for that which has no owner. Nobody owns the air we breathe, which is why it gets polluted. Somewhat less theoretically, the common can be seen as a park in a city. City parks are most often dirtier than private gardens. Many people visit the park and, quite simply, are a little more careless there, because the park does not belong to them. A property owner would presumably see to it that his garden was not littered with empty bottles and ice-cream wrappers. But the park is someone else's responsibility. It is jointly owned by the visitors, that is to say through the medium of the city's political administration (which, one hopes, the visitors have helped to elect).

Perhaps the dilemma of the common is not such a dangerous problem in the case of, say, a Stockholm park, but things get more serious if the same argument is applied to a vital resource like water. In parts of California's Mojave Desert, for example, water rights are linked to land ownership. Many landowners extract water from the same aquifer. Because water rights have not been regulated among the landowners themselves, many of them are extracting water in such quantities that the supply is dwindling. From the point of view of the individual landowner, it is of course rational to bag as much water as possible before the supply runs out. This could be termed "the tragedy of the common water." Lack of property rights, in other words, causes overexploitation. The solution to this problem is private water ownership. Technically the true substance of ownership can be hard to pin down, at least where water flowing in a watercourse is concerned. There are various ways of overcoming this problem, but that is too technical an issue for our present purpose.[45]

Chile introduced private ownership of water, with very good results. At the beginning of the 1980s the Chilean government granted farmers, companies, and local authorities the right to own local water. This enabled them to sell it in a free market, and the effects have been outstanding. Water supply has grown faster than in any other country. Thirty years ago only 27 percent of Chileans in rural areas and 63 percent in urban communities had steady access to safe water. Today's figures are 94 and 99 percent respectively—the highest for all the world's medium-income nations.[46]

The Chilean success story can be attributed to several factors, such as prices matching the true cost of water and positive economic development in general.[47] But the most important reform was the introduction of the right to own water and to buy and sell it at freely determined prices.

Trade in water increased people's access to water in two ways:

- The amount of water available increased, because the owners (farmers) now had a strong incentive to avoid spillage and produce and deliver as much as possible. The more they sold, the more money they made.
- The price of water fell, because the introduction of water rights led to a far-reaching decentralization of water management, thereby improving efficiency and reducing waste. In addition, the growth of supply put downward pressure on prices.

Farmers can often save water by using more efficient techniques of irrigation. Drip irrigation, for example, is more efficient than the traditional method. Only half the water used by the world's farmers generates any food. Most of Chile's new fruit farmers use water-saving irrigation techniques. Farmers can also switch to crops requiring less water. There is huge room for improvement here.

But farmers were not alone in husbanding water resources more carefully. When EMOS, Chile's largest water utility (publicly owned at the time but since privatized), realized that it could no longer get water free of charge but would have to buy it from the owners, it invested in a program for heavily reducing wastage.

But the introduction of clearly defined and tradable water rights is not only conducive to greater efficiency, it also results in the water going where it does the most economic good, which in turn spells greater prosperity. Water that cannot be traded is pent up in the use that politicians have determined for it. Its yield is then suboptimized and the whole country left so much the poorer. It is quite common in poor countries for big farmers with good water supplies to grow water-intensive crops instead of those needing less water. In the latter case they could sell the surplus, for example, to industry. But you can't sell what doesn't belong to you.

If farmers can sell their water at prices freely negotiated with the buyers, some of them will sell it for more useful purposes, such as to other farmers or to nearby towns and cities. With farmers selling their surplus water, other farmers will have a chance of growing, less expensively, the crops they want to grow. And the market will see to it that the water is sold to more efficient growers, thereby enhancing the prosperity of the nation as a whole.

Chilean agriculture has accomplished a massive transformation, thanks to the trade in water. Most important, it has moved from low-value activities, such as cattle-farming and cultivation of cereals and oleaginous plants to fruit and wine production, which is much more lucrative. Between 1975 and 1990, without any major infrastructure investments being made, Chile raised its agricultural productivity by 6 percent annually, and today it is the world's largest exporter of winter fruit to the Northern Hemisphere.[48]

Water that is sold to a city instead of to another farmer will be used either by industry or by private individuals. Both cases mean good business for the farmer. Industry produces more value for the same water input, and private persons are ready to pay more for the water than the farmer can earn from crops. Either way, the price will be adjusted in such a way that the water goes where it will do the most good. The net gains of trading in rights can equal, or be several times greater than, the value of the rights themselves.[49]

Trade also benefits urban dwellers. The Chilean city of La Serena, for example, has for years now been able to keep up with rising demand by purchasing water from farmers in outlying areas far more cheaply than if the city's taxpayers had been forced to finance the dam construction project originally planned.

Another advantage is that farmers owning the water they need for agriculture are not at the mercy of the public sector and its sometimes capricious pricing and imposition of quotas on water. Farmers with direct control of water are better able to plan their activities.

The fact is that spontaneous trading in water rights occurs quite frequently, even when the law does not really allow it. In India, for example, several states—Gujarat not least among them—have quite advanced informal water markets. The profits from this trade have been estimated at $1.38 billion annually. The problem, though, is that the trade is illegal, or rather, informal. The government, perceiving its advantages, has opted for non-intervention and has turned a blind eye. But the informality of the trade means that there is no one to ensure that agreements are adhered to. This situation has given rise to tensions and efficiency losses. So it is better to acknowledge and legitimize the trade, thereby creating water rights that can be legally asserted and provide secure, straightforward rules of conduct. Trade is then made easier.

Pakistan is another example. A survey by the Pakistani Water and Power Development Authority revealed water trading in 70 percent of the watercourses investigated. In places where the trade had been legalized, farmers' incomes had risen by 40 percent.[50]

As a third example we can take the Crocodile River in Mpuma-
langa, South Africa, where, historically, political control of water
resources has had severe social, economic, and environmental consequences. But during a heavy drought in the early 1990s, the
farmers began trading illegally in their water rights. Events showed
that they were ready to pay up to three times the price officially
set by the government. In this way, the water ended up where it
did the most good and was used more efficiently. Much of the
water shortage was remedied as a result. The authorities, perceiving
the benefits of the water trade, eventually legalized it. Not only
did this trade help farmers to weather a severe drought, it was also
a stroke of fortune in purely economic terms. The net profit on
the water trade is estimated at 25 million South African rands. As
another positive effect of the water trade, plans could be shelved
for building a great dam that would otherwise have cost 230 million
rands of taxpayers' money.[51]

Other developing countries—Mexico and Brazil, for example—
have lately introduced successful water rights reforms.

As mentioned at the beginning of the chapter, problems from
lack of formally recognized property rights and water do not only
occur when the rights refer to water, but also to land. In fact, the
lack of land titling in many of the informal settlements in the cities
of developing countries is an important explanation for the fact
that poor households are not connected to water and sewerage
networks, notably in Manila. First, bureaucratic impediments such
as lack of formal addresses, registration, and documentation make
it difficult for any provider, private or public, both to extend the
network and to bill customers. Second, sometimes suppliers are
forbidden by law from serving these settlements, since that would
imply a formal recognition of them. Third, since shantytowns and
other informal settlements are not formally recognized or registered, they often fail to be included in the contract between the
government and the private firm.[52]

Property rights to water have a very positive effect on its use and protection. The ability to trade helps to achieve the highest possible yield. This system, furthermore, can help to maximize the number of people having access to clean, safe water, as in Chile. Water trading can also play a role in averting conflicts, which is the subject of the next chapter.

CHAPTER FIVE

Markets and Conflicts

Mark Twain is alleged to have once said, "Whiskey is for drinking; water is for fighting over," meaning that when an asset is scarce and its ownership unclear, conflicts often develop over it that can lead to violence. Water, necessary for survival even in the short term, is probably more likely to be fought over than any other resource. Furthermore, water is often a tool in conflicts, not least when people are short of it.

Conflicts over water have beset the world for thousands of years. As pointed out by Peter Gleick, one of the world's foremost water experts, "There is a long and highly informative history of conflicts and tensions over water resources, the use of water systems as weapons during war, and the targeting of water systems during conflicts caused by other factors."[53] In his *Water Conflict Chronology*, Gleick outlines hundreds of water-related conflicts, starting with Sumerian legends and biblical tales from as early as 3000 B. C. and ending with terrorist attacks against water supply systems in Baghdad in 2003. Between these instances, he mentions everything from Arizona military maneuvers along the border with California in the 1930s to military action in the Balkans in the 1990s.[54]

Overall, during the past 50 years, 507 interstate conflict situations worldwide, including 21 cases of outright hostilities, have arisen from disagreements over water.[55] During the 1990s there were armed conflicts over water in Bangladesh, Tadzhikistan, Malaysia, Yugoslavia, Angola, East Timor, Namibia, Botswana, Zambia, Ecuador, and Peru.[56]

In modern times, nowhere has water played a more important role in a conflict than in the Middle East. The Six-Day War fought by Israel against Syria, Jordan, and Egypt was in part concerned with a water dispute. Israel refused to evacuate the Golan Heights and the West Bank, in part because the country would lose its control of water flows and expose thousands of Israelis to the risk of being deprived of water.

An agreement on water from the Jordan River loomed large in the peace treaty that Israel and Jordan concluded in 1994. Former Egyptian president Anwar Sadat said in 1979 that water was the only issue that could force Egypt to go to war again.[57] Egypt also has problems to the south. The country gets 85 percent of its fresh water from the Nile, and Ethiopia is planning to increase its extraction of water from that river.

Indeed, water is often a source of conflict. And it is more likely to be so in the future. "The wars of the 21st century will be fought over water," Ishmael Serageldin, a former vice president of the World Bank and chairman of the World Commission on Water, has famously stated. And he is not the only one to make such predictions. In fact, there is plenty of talk about future "water wars."

From a post–Cold War perspective, competition for global dominance is no longer the main threat to our security. Next to international terrorism, differing views and interests regarding access to, and control over, natural resources such as water may actually be one of the main factors behind instability and hostilities. Particularly tricky are cases where one river, or river system, provides water to many nations, some of which may be steadfast political or ideological opponents. But there can be conflicts even between countries with otherwise excellent relations if they have the same watercourse as their principal source of water supply. If one country starts emptying the river, less will be left over for the countries downstream. Countries like Egypt, Hungary, Botswana, Cambodia, and Syria all derive more than 75 percent of their water from rivers flowing through other countries first.[58]

However, conflicts over water do not only, or even perhaps primarily, arise between countries. Hostilities between provinces, municipalities, different economic actors, and groups in society may be even more important.

Time and time again, the various federal states of India have been embroiled in disputes with one another over access to water from rivers and dams. An Indian lawyer has prophesied: "Water disputes, if not attended to, will become a major headache for the stability of Indian society."[59]

Against this background, it is all the more important that we do all we can to ensure that water is handled carefully, that it is used as effectively as possible, that it ends up where it will be most effectively used, and that as many people as possible are able to acquire the water they need. Then the risks of war over water can be significantly diminished. Here, markets and the private sector have an important role to play.

Water corporations are more likely than government bureaucracies to handle water with care. Profit motives give them strong incentives to conserve water and to see to it that their customers are served rather than water being spilled. Furthermore, trading will guarantee maximum output of water. Also, clearly defined and recognized property rights to water can lower the risk of conflicts. Another advantage is that markets and private providers are more likely to reach more people with water pipes, lowering the risk of conflicts caused by water stress. Last but not least, monetizing a good can make it less political.

Hillel Shuval, professor of environmental sciences at the Hebrew University of Jerusalem, maintains that water-related tensions between Israel and the Palestinians abated only after Israel agreed to sell water to the Palestinians. Trade in water, he says,

> . . . ensures rationalization of water use [and] if you monetize the conflict, it makes it less emotional. If water is seen as a commodity, not as mother's milk, it shows that there is not enough there to go to war. [60]

The point Professor Shuval makes is that when countries trade water with each other, the liquid is less likely to cause conflicts. When water can be acquired by means other than force, these means are likely to be used. Trading could therefore help avert tensions and ensure that all parties involved can acquire the share they need instead of taking and controlling water by force. Of course, giving the market and private sector a greater role in the water sector would not be a universal cure for wars, but it would certainly reduce the causes of conflict in many places.

Let us illustrate with the city of Warangal in the Indian state of Andhra Pradesh. Warangal has a problem with people stealing water from the canal that is its main source of water supply. Farmers quite simply divert water from the canal to enormous areas beyond surveillance. As a result the city's water supply is constantly threatened, and the local authorities constantly have to negotiate with central authorities for a bigger allocation from the dam that feeds the canal. The city also builds small dams of sandbags, which are then removed by people dependent on the water downstream.

The farmers really have no choice but to steal water. The politically determined allocation is insufficient for their needs, and they have no possibility of buying water, because there is no such thing as a water market. But in other parts of India the appearance of tradable water rights has made water legally procurable. Added to which the water trade has led to more efficient use and, consequently, less shortage, which in turn reduces tensions and the likelihood of conflict.

It should be noted, though, that there is a growing body of research arguing that the threat of conflict over water is exaggerated. First, some academics claim that very rarely have there been outright wars between states over water. States also develop ways to handle international water conflicts through international treaties and diplomacy, not least between countries sharing the same water or with a potential conflict of interest over a source.[61]

There are strong arguments against this view. First, future security concerns are not likely to be primarily about war in the traditional sense, with one sovereign state being involved in armed conflict with another. Therefore, the claim that water is rarely the sole cause of *war* is not that relevant. It certainly is the cause of other disruptions of peace, as shown by the Gleick chronology just mentioned. Furthermore, even if water will not be the *sole* cause of conflict, it will certainly be an important contributing factor. Lastly, similar points about the role of international cooperation in inhibiting war have been put forward by peace researchers in general (not dealing primarily with water-related conflicts) for decades. And despite their scholarly work, along with an abundance of international treaties, military conflicts have not been avoided. Therefore it is not certain, or even likely, that peace research in relation to water will be any more successful.

Handling water with greater care is thus also important in maintaining peace. The market and business have an important role to play in this regard.

CHAPTER SIX

The Price of Water

Now we come to the heart of the matter: how much can water be allowed to cost? This is the hottest issue in the whole discussion concerning water privatization in poor countries. Opponents of private involvement claim that poor people will be unable to afford sufficient water if prices are set by the market instead of by politicians. Privatization, they maintain, leads automatically to higher prices. This is the argument underlying much of the resistance to admitting commercial interests to the distribution of water in poor countries. Greater scope for the market and the private sector, we are told, will augment still further the current statistic of more than a billion people without adequate access to water, bringing greater poverty, diseases, and death.

A group of researchers, who work on behalf of Public Service International, an international union of public servants, maintain in one report that

> high prices and disconnections must mean that the poorest segments of society are likely to be the main losers from the privatization process. Where this increases use of unsafe water sources, the consequences will be disastrous for public health.[62]

Another report expresses the argument as follows:

> The winners in privatization of water are private companies. . . . Poor households are the main losers.[63]

In our mind's eye, we see girls forced to trek for miles and miles every day with heavy jars on their heads, children who have to work instead of going to school, millions of people dying of diarrheal dehydration, and multinational corporations profiting hand over fist by the thirst of the impoverished. Images like this arouse strong feelings and offer easy arguments, but just how truthful and relevant are they? Is this the real outcome of market pricing and privatization? Or are the opponents of privatization so blinded by their detestation of the market economy and big business that they put dogmas and ideology before the best interests of the poor?

There are strong indications that wide scope for enterprise and the market are vital for supplying clean, safe water to the billion and more people who at present are without it. People without mains water are paying far more for their water today than they would if connected to a distribution network. Higher prices give the water distributor both the resources and the incentive to connect more households to the main supply network. Those who are without water today would thus benefit greatly from a rise in the price of mains water. Moreover, they spend a lot of time fetching water, which in itself is a heavy expense to them. It is these people's costs that are relevant to the comparison. Then again, unduly low prices have created both the capital shortage mentioned earlier and wastage, overuse, and inflexibility. They also deprive distributors of incentives for reaching new users. Last but not least, existing water use subsidies mostly benefit groups other than the very poorest.

Let us take a closer look at this matter. We can start with the question of water supply and demand, going on from there to see whether market prices are higher or lower than politically determined prices and, finally, whether privatization makes prices go up or down.

When the market is allowed to put a price on a good, it is supply and demand that decide it. Equilibrium occurs when supply and demand meet at a certain price level. Supply and demand are both disrupted when the price of a good is politically regulated. If the price set is lower than the equilibrium price, supply will diminish and demand increase. Conversely, if the price exceeds the equilibrium level, supply will increase and demand diminish. This is basic economics that people are taught in high school, and so it is strange indeed that the argument should have such a tenuous foothold in discussions of world water supply.

The big problem regarding the price of water in poor parts of the world is that it is too low for supply and demand to converge. Instead of water being made to bear its own costs, the production and distribution of it are subsidized out of taxation revenue.[64] No less than $45 billion a year is spent on subsidizing water in the Third World. In developing countries, the price of water is so low that on average it covers only about 30 percent of the water supplier's expenses. Some experts estimate that the water sector is subsidized by an average of about 80 percent of expenses.[65]

If not even current expenditure or working expenses are covered, there will be even less money to spare for maintenance and infrastructure investments to improve the distribution or quality of the water, and the supply network cannot possibly be enlarged in order to serve those who at present are without safe water.

Equally important, perhaps, is the determination of the water distributor to reach as many users as possible. If the price of water is so low that extending the supply network to new users costs more than the distributor can expect to recoup by means of charges, there is very little reason indeed why the distributor should want to enlarge the network at all, still less make the extra effort required in making such connections. Why invest in a guaranteed loss-maker?

For political reasons, the price of water is simply too low, the object of this being to make sure that everybody can afford the water they need. But in practice, we have a situation where supply is too low to reach the poor, with the effect that more than a billion poor people have to pay through the nose for poor-quality water, thereby risking disease and death. Excessively low prices go a long way toward accounting for the inadequate supply of clean, safe water in poor countries. From a supply perspective, then, there are strong reasons for not influencing the price of water by political means, be it through regulations or subsidies, and instead allowing the market to decide. Some NGOs seem to have realized this. At the People's World Water Forum that took place in Mumbai, India, in January 2004, Prakash Amatya, a Nepalese NGO worker, complained that "[t]he water shortage in Kathmandu is because water is almost free."[66]

But supply is not the only thing affected by price controls. If the price of water is politically set below the market price, demand will also become excessive, with a number of unfortunate consequences.

First, water will be wasted. Users have fewer incentives for economizing or limiting their use of water if it is too cheap. In the home, for example, no one stops to consider whether to use the same water for two loads of wash or whether more than one child can use the same bath water. The big savings, though, are to be made in agriculture, a point we shall be revisiting. Wastage helps to cause both water shortage and environmental destruction. The problem of waste becomes graver still when instead of water being quantitatively priced, the user pays a fixed charge. That completely eliminates any incentives for economizing.

South Korea offers a blatant example of water wastage. In 2002, when the country was experiencing a shortage of water, it emerged that South Koreans use more water per capita than any other OECD nation, despite their income level being one of the lowest. Water was heavily subsidized, and so wasting it cost very little. Compounding the complexities and vagaries of water management, the water bureaucracy numbered no less than five different public authorities.[67]

In Windhoek, the capital of Namibia, both informational campaigns and pricing have been deployed in a bid to curb water consumption. Price modifications proved very effective, reducing water consumption by 20 percent, whereas public education measures achieved only a 5 percent reduction.[68]

Industrial and agricultural use of water is even more important than domestic consumption. Between them, industry and agriculture account for 92 percent of world water consumption, and so this is where the big savings are to be made.[69] But they have little incentive for reducing their consumption when water is underpriced.

Farmers, who account for 70 percent of the world's water consumption, are often hugely uneconomical about it.[70] For example, in growing water-intensive crops they derive a less-than-optimal nutrition content from a given quantity of water. Agriculture, in fact, is one of the real villains of the global water drama. The less developed a country is, the larger the proportion of its water is consumed by agriculture. So more efficient water use in agriculture will have the greatest effect in poor countries.

Half the water used by the world's farmers generates no food. Minor changes, therefore, can result in much water being saved. A 10 percent improvement in the distribution of water to agriculture would double the world's potable water supply. Here is another example: Tomato growing by traditional irrigation requires 40 percent more water than with drip irrigation. The water needed to grow rice on one hectare of land would keep 100 rural households supplied for four years.[71] If water costs what it is really worth, instead of being subsidized, farmers are very likely to make investments aimed at reducing the amount of water needed for food production.

One very clear example of the perverse effects of mistaken water pricing comes from California. Heavy subsidies give farmers a copious supply of water at very low prices. Urban dwellers pay nearly a thousand times as much for their water as farmers do. And so rice is grown in the desert, a water-guzzling enterprise, at the same time that Californian cities are spending huge sums of money on desalination plants converting sea water into fresh water. [72] Bad water policy, then, is not confined to developing countries but also exists in highly developed countries with effective systems of government.

The demand aspect thus also argues against controlling the price of water by political means. But, the advocates of politicized water pricing would object, it is humanitarian aspects that matter most, not questions of supply and demand. Let us then consider these aspects, which are the main focus of this book.

This brings us to the question of whether the poor can afford water at market prices. Opponents of market prices for water maintain that if the market is allowed to set the price of water, this will make it difficult or impossible for poor people to obtain as much water as they need. How true is this? It depends on the kind of comparison we choose to make.

First, though, it has to be made clear that a distinction ought to be made between discussing political versus market-driven pricing and, on the other hand, discussing private versus public water. These are two different issues. Placing water distribution in private hands does not necessarily mean the price will be determined by the market. There is nothing to stop politicians from still controlling the price of water supplied under private auspices. As we shall see later on, privatized and completely deregulated water régimes are few and far between. Instead, prices are most often determined politically, even after commercial interests have become involved. The most common arrangement is for the price to be inscribed in the contract drawn up between the public authority and the private player when the latter is admitted to the business of water distribution.

When discussing poor people's access to water, the only reasonable starting point must be the billion-plus people with no access to safe water. There is a strong connection between development in terms of GDP and access to water. Most often it is the very poorest people in poor countries who are without water and are not served by existing water distribution networks. UN-Habitat has described in a number of case studies and extensive data how poor segments of the population in the cities of the developing world are grossly overrepresented among the people who suffer from lack of access to water and sanitation. One study of 15 countries with low and medium-low incomes showed more than 80 percent of the poorest quarter of the population to be without water.[73]

The most common way for poor city-dwellers in developing countries to obtain water is by purchasing it from small-time vendors in kiosks, or those who either have a local well (with often polluted water) or deliver water by motor vehicle or by some other means. Contractors often drive tankers to poor districts, selling water by the can, in which case the very poorest of the world's inhabitants are already exposed to market forces but on very unfair terms, because water obtained like this is on average twelve times more expensive than water from regular water mains, and often still more expensive than that.[74] (See table 6.1.) This is a very important point that tends to be completely ignored by anti-privatization activists.

The poorest, then, are mainly unaffected by any increases in the price of mains water. Instead, more than a billion of the world's poor are suffering from the very high prices charged for the water

Table 6.1. The price of water from alternative sources, in relation to mains water.

Region/Country	City	x times more costly
Africa		
Mauritania	Nouakchott	1-100
Nigeria	Onitsha	6-38
	Lagos	4-10
Kenya	Nairobi	7-11
Togo	Lomé	7-10
Asia		
Pakistan	Karachi	28-83
Indonesia	Surabaya	20-60
	Jakarta	4-60
Bangladesh	Dacca	12-25
Latin America		
Honduras	Tegucigalpa	16-34
Ecuador	Guayaquil	20
Peru	Lima	17

Source: Moor (1997).

they are forced to rely on for lack of water pipes. But they are indirectly affected, in a very positive way. In fact, they would gain a great deal from market pricing of water, because the supplier would then have both the capital and the incentive to extend the water supply network to include those who are not connected at present, that is, the very poorest inhabitants of the poor countries. They would then get better water at lower prices than before.

For example, in Port-au-Prince, the capital of Haiti, people with mains water supply pay $1 per m³, whereas those lacking a main water connection pay $10 for the same amount. So the poor of Port-au-Prince would benefit from a price rise, even if water were made as much as nine times more expensive.[75] The same goes for most other Third World cities. In Vientiane, Laos, informal vendor water costs 136 times more than network water; in Ulan Bator, Mongolia, it costs 35 times more; and in Bandung, Indonesia, as much as 489 times more.[76] Unserved populations in these cities all stand to benefit from higher prices for mains water.

There are also survey reports showing that poor people in the developing countries are ready to pay more for their water than they are paying at present.[77] Other surveys show that price elasticity, that is, the sensitivity of consumption to rising prices, is lower in households than in agriculture and industry.[78] This, it might be argued, is only natural, since the consequences of being without water are direr for people than for farmers and industry. But on the other hand this confirms the possibility of conserving water by means of higher prices, since, as we saw earlier, agriculture and industry account for 92 percent of the world's water consumption.

There are good examples of cities where higher prices have had very salutary effects. In Bogor, Indonesia, prices were substantially raised and the utility was able to connect more households to the main supply network, giving a greater number of poor people access to cheaper water. In Tegucigalpa, the capital of Honduras, groups of poor precincts joined force and signed an agreement with the water utility whereby the consumers themselves were to pay for the mains connection. Eighty-five percent of all households bought the connection and in this way had water brought to their homes, at the same time reducing their expenditure on water.[79]

Another aspect to bear in mind when discussing the price of water from the viewpoint of the poor is the costs they already incur by not having access to piped water. As we saw in chapter 2, hundreds of millions of people spend several hours a day fetching water. During that time they can neither work nor study, and so they lose earnings. These losses are hard to quantify, but it would seem to be a reasonable supposition that several hours of unpaid, low-productive work a day means heavy losses, both to the individuals themselves and to the community as a whole. A study from Dehra Dun, a city in northern India, shows that if the price of water is made to include the time that people (as usual, mostly poor people) spend fetching water, and if to this we add the loss of earnings for that length of time, then in reality the water costs 15 times its nominal price.[80] This is a crucial factor when discussing the price of water.

Once again, then, the poor would benefit from higher prices. Besides, public subsidies mainly benefit more privileged groups. Public water utilities cover only 30 percent of their costs. The remaining 70 percent is made up with subsidies from taxation revenue. Those who at present do not have access to any mains supply network are not reached by any subsidies either. In certain developing countries, between 80 and 90 percent of the wealthiest fifth of the population have access to publicly distributed water, as against only 30 to 50 percent or less of the poorest fifth. In Colombia, for example, 80 percent of all beneficiaries of water subsidies are people in medium and high income brackets. A study of six Central American cities showed that it was mainly the wealthiest 60 percent who were reached by subsidies.[81] In practice, then, it is mainly the well-to-do, such as the middle class and farmers, who benefit. They do not really have any need of cheaper water and could very well pay a lot more for it.

As UN-Habitat puts it:

> Low-income urban dwellers are often paying high prices for very inadequate water provision—for instance, purchasing water from vendors at 2–50 times the price per liter paid by higher-income groups, who receive heavily subsidized water piped into their homes.[82]

In Chile, however, water subsidies have targeted the very poorest. Because water is self-financing, the majority of people pay the true cost of it, while extremely poor people are given a reduced rate. South Africa has a different system, but based on a similar principle, namely that of giving the poorest citizens access to water without encouraging overconsumption. All families are entitled to 25 liters of water daily, free of charge, while volumes in excess of that amount are a good deal more expensive.[83] But the South African model entails two problems. First, subsidies benefit everyone, not just the poor; and second, water utilities have little incentive for extending the water supply system to poor people who are not expected to consume much.

It also has to be remembered that clean, safe water cannot be produced and delivered without expense. Someone has to pay for it. Subsidies are expenditure that the state finances out of taxation revenue contributed by the population. Those who benefit from subsidized water, then, are to a great extent the people who also pay for the benefit, albeit indirectly. The only people who pay for the subsidies without deriving any benefit from them are in fact the very poorest, who do not have access to mains water.

Chile's former secretary for agriculture, Renato Gazmuri, points out that the former Chilean system of state-subsidized water actually implied a regressive redistribution of wealth. Since low-income earners consume a larger portion of their income than the well-to-do, a larger part of their income goes to taxes (consumption being taxed more heavily than savings and investments). And since low-income earners consume less water and thus obtain a smaller share of the subsidies, water subsidies in practice imply a transfer of resources from the poor to the better-off. The middle class gets cheap water and the poor foot the bill.[84]

Andrew Nickson, who has written a report on the subject for the UK Department for International Development (DFID), aptly summarizes the whole matter as follows:

> The publicly-operated water sector in low and middle-income countries is failing to meet the needs of the urban poor. Instead it has ended up subsidizing the convenience interests of the rich.[85]

This being so, the money spent on making up the deficits of public water utilities would be better spent on direct cash support or other assistance to those in need of it.

The cost of subsidies directed at the Chilean poor amounts to $40 million. The general subsidies were costing no less than $100 million, that is, more than twice as much. The difference has been applied to more pressing concerns, such as measures to combat poverty.

Another way of helping underprivileged households when subsidies vanish is by distributing water vouchers that entitle them to a certain level of water consumption and for which the water utility then invoices the state. Where feasible, this is probably the best way of guaranteeing that poor households can afford the basic amount of necessary water, while at the same time making sure that the operators get the capital and incentive to reach the poor with their networks.

The debate on the price of water and subsidies ties in with the sociological discussion concerning insiders and outsiders. One group is left outside a system while another is inside it. Relations between these groups are usually complicated. As regards the price of water, it is the poorest—those not connected to water mains— who are the outsiders, while those whose households receive piped water are the insiders. Our outsiders are most in need of being inside the system. They incur far heavier expense than they would if they were inside, and also far heavier expense than those who are insiders today. But the insiders will not let them in, because that would mean greater expense for themselves. What we have, then, is a conflict of interest between the relatively well-off middle class and the marginalized poor. It seems odd that so many leftist NGOs in effect side with the affluent.

We have now discussed the necessity of higher prices and the advantages of market pricing. So does "privatization" mean higher prices? As has already been remarked, there is a vital distinction to be made between market prices and privatization.

Once again, it needs to be said that the people we must take as our starting point in this discussion are the billion or more who at present have no mains water supply and who pay heavily for their water in both money and time. Their water, on average, is 12 times more expensive than mains water, and generally of poorer quality. These people will pay a lower price if they are connected to the main water supply. But what about those who are connected already? Will they have to pay more or less? This is a tricky question, to which there is no simple answer.

There are arguments maintaining that prices will rise, just as there are other arguments maintaining that they will go down. In reality, there are examples of prices both rising and falling following the admission of commercial interests. In three of the cases we shall be reviewing in chapters 7 and 8, prices went up after privatization, and in three others prices went down. Price effects hinge on several factors.

One reason for expecting prices to rise is that any public subsidies will disappear once commercial interests are admitted. It would be quite possible to go on subsidizing water distribution by transferring funds to the private firm, but usually this does not happen, because one reason for governments transferring water distribution to private enterprises is that they are short of resources and want to cut costs and use public funds for different purposes. Moreover, there is a risk of the subsidies being constructed in such a way that the private water utility will not profit by reaching as many users as possible, which in turn eliminates one of the strongest benefits of private involvement, namely incentives for extending the water supply network to those excluded from it under the public régime. But the strongest argument of all against subsidized water is that the support does not get through to those who need it most.

Disregarding subsidies, though, is it still more expensive to entrust water distribution to a private agency than to a public agency? There is one argument that speaks to this effect. Privatization is often associated with heavy investments. Lack of investment in the water sector of the developing counties is one of the main reasons for more than a billion people not having access to safe water. Private players are often admitted with a view to gaining access to their capital. And since water distribution should cover its own costs and the company wants earnings to exceed expenditure, the investments often make it necessary to raise the price of water. It is very uncommon for water to be so cheap to produce and distribute that public authorities can attract investors to reverse years of neglected investment needs and at the same time offer their customers a lower price than before.

On the other hand, the need for investment is unaffected by water being supplied under public or private auspices. A public supplier would also need to make the same big investments as a private one in order to connect as many users as possible to the system and to raise the quality of distribution. And there is nothing to suggest that costs would be lower merely because of the investments being made under public auspices; if anything, the opposite is the case. So the argument that privatization per se leads to investments, which lead to higher costs and, accordingly, to higher prices, does not "hold water." At least not if you are dissatisfied with the present state of things, with 12 million deaths a year owing to shortage of water.

In this connection, it is important to recognize that it is erroneous to view investments purely as a cost to the company and to users and the public sector. Nor is it certain that investments will lead to higher prices in the slightly longer term. Let us consider an example from another industry. When Volvo invests millions in a new car model, it counts on getting its money back. The new model is attractive in the eyes of customers, and so it sells well.

A new production line is more efficient than the old one, enabling cars to be sold for less. The customers get a car that appeals to them, and more people can afford it. Thanks to the growth of efficiency, the employees working on the new production line are more productive and can therefore be paid more (perhaps they have also undergone some kind of training), which in turn stimulates the economy around them. The public sector pulls in more taxation revenue from the company's profits and the employees' earnings and also from the purchases made by the new car owners. In short, everyone benefits.

Or consider an even clearer and perhaps more immediate example from the pharmaceutical industry. After investing heavily, a company invents a new drug that will enable thousands of people to recover their health and return to work, becoming a source of income instead of an item of expenditure to the public sector.

The same goes for water. In the longer term, investments lead to a growth of earnings and a fall in expenditure. Private enterprise reaches more users with fewer employees and at lower cost. This has a number of positive effects.

Ghanaian Hawa Amandu

Hawa Amandu lives in Maamobi, a slum district on the outskirts of Accra, the capital of Ghana. Where she lives there are no water pipes, no wells have been sunk, and there are no cisterns. Instead she has to walk just over a kilometer and a half, every day, to fetch water for which she pays somewhat more than 75 cents daily. That is the same price as for the average family in London, but Hawa's income is only a fraction of theirs. Sometimes she goes without food so that there will be water for her grandchildren to drink. If she had mains water it would cost less, she would be able to go out to work instead of carrying heavy loads of water, and she would have a better income. The Ghanaian government has now resolved on a major investment scheme in partnership with the private sector.

Source: Christian Aid (2002).

The very strongest argument against prices automatically rising when water is commercialized, however, lies in the superior efficiency of private enterprise compared with public production. As we saw in chapter 3, public water utilities have a number of built-in weaknesses, such as lack of competence for water and corporate management, distorted incentives, corruption, and political control. When a commercial utility comes in with economies of scale, more capital for efficiency investments, greater knowledge and experience, better technology, and fewer but better-trained employees, there is a potential for delivering water at a lower price and still making money from it. So there is no straight answer to the question of whether commercialization of water means higher or lower prices. Will the capital and competence of the private sector offset the loss of subsidies? As mentioned earlier, prices went up in three cases and down in three others out of the six privatizations we will be reviewing later on. But it is worth repeating that public authorities are still at liberty to control the price of water supplied privately. Privatization does not automatically lead to market pricing, and in fact it very rarely does so. The reasons for water being made to bear its own costs to a far greater extent than at present and for allotting market mechanisms a more prominent role in the pricing of water are nevertheless strong.

CHAPTER SEVEN

The Possibilities of Privatization

Many governments in developing countries, realizing that things cannot go on as they are, have begun looking for ways of improving their national water distribution. They cannot afford to wait until their countries attain a level of development at which mains water is supplied to the majority of citizens. They have come to realize that the widespread lack of clean, safe water is very much a result of the negative consequences of distribution being in public hands.

Accordingly, poor countries are increasingly turning to business enterprise for help with water distribution, but this has occurred on only a limited scale and did not get seriously underway until the 1990s. The fact is that only 3 percent of poor people in the developing world today get their water from private formal-sector suppliers. Private involvement in Third World water distribution, then, is very limited, which is a major problem given that $180 billion will be needed annually to make safe water universally available in the Third World.

Opponents of private involvement in poor countries tend to put a privatization label on all forms of entrepreneurial involvement in water distribution. No doubt the term "privatization" has a far-reaching pedagogic and demagogic impact. In fact, there are very few systems in the world today with completely privatized water assets and completely deregulated suppliers. Only a tiny proportion of the private investments made in the water sector in developing countries represent outright privatization. Most often they represent various forms of cooperation between public- and private-sector or government and business. These connections are frequently labeled water privatization.[86]

Different degrees of private involvement in water are classifiable into six different forms. The lowest degree of private involvement is the service contract, whereby, quite simply, a private contractor looks after the maintenance of existing networks. Another model is for a private firm to run the actual distribution of water but for the water and infrastructure to remain public property. This is rather like a company outsourcing its IT department. In both cases, the principals remain responsible and take the risk. A third way of involving private enterprise is by leasing out both water and infrastructure for a limited period.

A fourth method, known as BOOT (Build-Own-Operate-Transfer), usually involves a private company constructing or renovating the infrastructure, which it then leases for a fixed term. In concessions, the fifth alternative, a private distributor is allowed to rent available infrastructure but undertakes, as part of the contract, to achieve certain targets, for example concerning price, enlargement, or number of customers with access to water. A sixth possibility involves partially or wholly selling off rights and infrastructure to companies. Concession is the most common way of admitting private interests to water distribution.

If a further variable, controls, is added to the equation, one can, simplifying somewhat, distinguish between four traditional "water régimes":

- Publicly funded and administered water distribution (the most common arrangement worldwide).
- State-aided natural monopolies with price controls.
- State-aided natural monopolies with profit controls.
- State-controlled franchises, leasing or concession agreements.

Entirely free water markets with no public ownership or controls are thus very uncommon, so we will use the term "privatization" here as it is employed in the debate, namely in the sense of having various forms of commercial-interest involvement.

The private sector, as we have now seen, entered the water sector only quite recently. Companies are coming under increasing pressure to supply poor urban dwellers with the water they need. The reason why, up until now, water has mostly been under public management is that the market and private players were assumed to be incapable or unwilling to supply water to the poor. That was a mistaken assumption, for three reasons.

First, public administration has developed mechanisms whereby performance requirements in concessionary contracts include requiring companies to supply water to the poor. Second, companies have understood that the success of their operation in such a politicized environment as Third World cities depends on ensuring that water also gets through to the poor. Third, companies have perceived that water sales to the poor can be an important part of the market that they simply cannot afford to disregard. The poor, then, have great commercial value as consumers. Often they make up no less than 50 percent of a country's total market and thus cannot be ignored, politically or economically. So the challenge of supplying the poorest citizens with water is an integral part of corporate business planning. And, as shown in figure 7.1, companies have succeeded quite well in this respect.

In developing countries where private interests have invested in water and sanitation, 80 percent of the population on average have access to safe water, as against only 73 percent in developing countries with no private investments. The greater the involvement of the private sector in water supply, the greater the number of people with access to water.[87]

Figure 7.1. Access to safe water in developing countries respectively with and without private investment in water.[88]

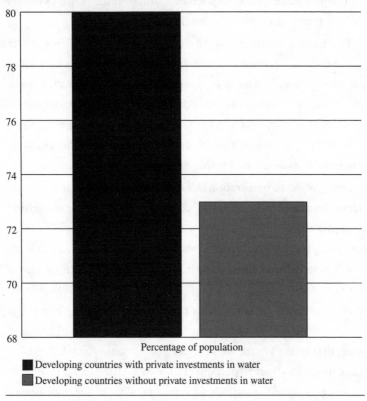

Percentage of population

■ Developing countries with private investments in water
■ Developing countries without private investments in water

Source: WDI online.

This is because private players do not share the weaknesses of public utilities. Private concerns generally have bigger investment resources, more competence for handling water and running an organization, access to newer and better technology, superior cost-awareness, and healthier incentive structures, added to which they are less bound by political dogmas and allegiances.

Privatization can very often serve to revitalize ossified systems. In many countries the water interest consists of producer interests, represented by politicians, trade unions, and the public supplier all working together hand in glove.[89] All these groups have an interest in perpetuating the status quo, thus giving rise to inflexibility and inefficiency. The advent of an external player in the form of a business enterprise often provides motivation for reforming sluggish bureaucracies and dissolving these problems.

The superior results achieved by private water distributors are also confirmed by a long line of studies, mostly of distributors in the industrialized world. The World Bank, though, has made a larger comparison between 50 water distributors in developing countries of Asia and the Pacific, showing private firms to be more efficient.[90]

Let us now consider some real-life cases and study the consequences of privatization and market adjustment of water régimes. We can start with Cambodia, where perhaps the clearest and most thorough comparison has been made between private and public water supply in a developing country.

Cambodia

Cambodia, like most other developing countries, has water distribution problems.[91] Privatization has therefore been tested. In three provincial cities, a private company was licensed to distribute water for three years. In a fourth city, no public resources were transferred. Instead, a private concern was granted permission to build a water supply network of its own in those outlying city districts that were not already served by the public water supply network. In the other 19 provincial cities, water distribution was entirely under public management.

Unfortunately, procurement in the first three cities was conducted without transparency, which left room for corruption and trade restraint, added to which the contracts were unclear as to what was required of the companies and on what terms their contracts would be renewable. Even so, the companies invested large sums of money in improving the water distribution system.

Cambodian politicians were of various minds as to whether the admission of commercial interests was a good or a bad thing, and so a survey was carried out, comparing water supply in the four cities with private involvement with that in four other cities where the supply remained public. The findings were unambiguous. Distribution worked better in the cities where commercial interests had been admitted.

Households in the cities with private water distribution were far more satisfied with the distributors' service than those in cities with public water utilities. Availability was better, in the sense of there being water in the faucets more often. All but one of the towns with private distribution had water on tap 24 hours a day. In cities with public distribution, water was available for between 8 and 12 hours a day. Cities with private water systems also had fewer disruptions of supply and better-quality water.

There were several reasons for the superiority of the private distributors. First, they had better-qualified, better-paid personnel. Second, their network maintenance was more regular, and they introduced programs for carefully monitoring the quality of the water. Last but not least, the private distributors were more strongly motivated to pursue customer satisfaction. So the strong points of private water distributors in Cambodia were very much an inversion of the weaknesses of public water utilities in developing countries: corporate management, quality-awareness, and incentives for uninterruptedly supplying good-quality water to as many people as possible.

True, the price of water was somewhat higher in cities with private water, but the difference was barely 6 percent. This slight difference was more than offset by the benefit of a regular domestic supply of safe water. What is more, the private distributors issued receipts for the greater part of their earnings, which leads one to suspect that the public utilities had a certain amount of income that went unreported, and that the real price of the water supplied by them was higher than officially stated.

Guinea

Guinea offers one of the earliest and most widely noticed instances of a poor country admitting private interests to its water sector.[92] In 1989, when water management in the cities was handed over to a private company, little more than two Guinean urban dwellers in 10 had access to clean, safe water. Twelve years later, in 2001, the figure was no fewer than seven in 10 (see figure 7. 2). The welfare benefit from privatization has been estimated at no less than $23 million.[93]

It is astonishing that the number of people with access to clean, safe water should have risen so dramatically in little more than a decade. Changes of this kind have been seen in countries developing very rapidly, but this is not the case with Guinea, which is a very poor country. Much of its economic growth has been eaten up by a growing population and servicing of the national debt. Instead the remarkable improvement can be put down to the private company, unlike Guinea's government and civil service, having the capital, competence, and incentive to deliver clean, safe water to as many people as possible. This is precisely what tends to distinguish private distributors from public ones.

Guinea is well off for water. It is estimated to have 166 billion m³ renewable water, although many of its water sources are shared with other countries. But the end of the 1980s found its national water supply in complete disarray. As illustrated in figure 7.2, only 23 percent of the urban population had access to clean, safe water. Only 10 of the country's three cities had water mains. In Conakry, the capital, the situation was critical. The population was increasing rapidly, and people's needs could not be met by the public distributor.

Figure 7.2. Access to clean, safe water in Guinea, with water supplied under public and private auspices respectively. Percentages of the urban population.

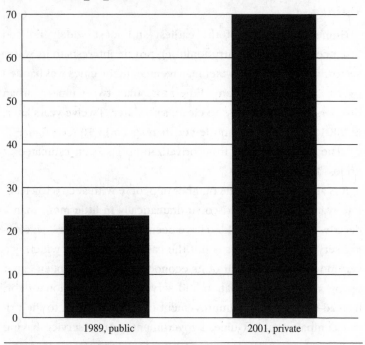

Source: Utrikesdepartementet (Swedish Ministry for Foreign Affairs) (2003a).

According to Ménard and Clarke, "Despite substantial loans from international donors, coverage was low and many non-connected residents drank water from polluted wells. Because of this, water-borne diseases were the main cause of death of infants and children and there were periodic cholera epidemics. The public enterprise responsible for the sector, the Entreprise National de Distribution de l'Eau Guinéenne (DEG), was poorly managed, overstaffed and practically insolvent."[94] It was able to produce only about 25 m^3 per inhabitant annually. There were only 12,000 connections (end-user pipes) in the whole country, and of these only 5 percent were fitted with meters (see table 7.1).

Table 7.1. Water in Guinea before and after private investment.

	Before	After
Urban dwellers with access to clean, safe water, percent	38	70
Cities with water mains, number	10	18
Water production in the capital, m³ per annum	40,000	100,000
End-user water pipes, number	12,000	30,500

Source: Utrikesdepartementet (Swedish Ministry for Foreign Affairs) (2003a).

The reasons for this situation, once again, were lack of resources and administrative ineptitude. Guinea's bureaucratic weaknesses were perhaps even more conspicuous than Cambodia's. The allocation of responsibilities among various authorities was unclear, water management was fragmented, and civil service efficiency was very poor.

In 1989, a public–private partnership (PPP),[95] funded with credits supported and underwritten by the World Bank, was formed by a national water utility and a private water company. The national utility, which has greater autonomy and flexibility than the civil service, is tasked with planning, running, and owning the water infrastructure. This is then leased to the private company, which collects payment from users in the form of connection and consumption charges.

It must be said that this PPP has not run altogether smoothly and that not all the project targets have been achieved. But there have been dramatic improvements. Delays and cost overruns on various construction projects were substantially reduced. The water supply network has been extended to more cities, and the number of connections has risen steeply. The proportion of urban dwellers with access to clean, safe water has nearly tripled, and Conakry's water production has doubled.

Everyone in Conakry seems to agree also that the quality of the water was superior after privatization—the general public, the World Health Organization, and local consumer organizations, as well as the manager of the local Coca-Cola plant (who should have quite deep knowledge of the matter). The effect, then, has been quite the opposite of that alleged by the detractors of commercial-interest involvement.[96]

Clearly, the private firm's superior water-management competence has made a big difference. And little wonder. A multinational corporation with years of experience of water distribution in both industrialized and developing countries is bound to be better at it than a public administration in a small, impoverished African country.

Privatization in Guinea boosted efficiency tremendously. The fact of 95 percent of all end-user pipes now having meters enables the company to collect payment for the water supplied. In this way the company earns money and can pay the rent for the infrastructure to the government, which in turn can use the rent money for investments in infrastructure, both new and old. More and more people gain better and better access to clean, safe water.

The question of water pricing is bound up with incentives. The price paid for water in Guinea, by the few people connected to the public water mains, was heavily subsidized. In other words, it was so low that the proceeds from water sales did not cover costs. And so the system was badly run, the existing infrastructure was poorly maintained, and there was a shortage of investment capital for reaching more users. Since the investment, the price of water has gone up quite a lot, from 15 cents per m^3 in 1989 to almost a dollar in 2000. To offset these price rises, a sliding-scale subsidization scheme was introduced, which was phased out in 1995.

The most important point in the pricing discussion, however, is that before privatization the majority of Guineans had no access to mains water at all. They do now. And for these people, the cost of water has fallen drastically. The moral issue, then, is whether it was worth raising the price for the minority of people already connected before privatization in order to reach the 70 percent connected today. Given the dreadful consequences of being without clean, safe water, this question can only be answered in the affirmative.[97]

Gabon

Some opponents of private involvement in water supply in poor countries concede that it may have had positive effects in a few Third World cities. But, it is argued, the majority of people in poor countries who are short of water live in rural areas, where urban logic does not apply. Distances are far greater than in the towns and cities, and lack of infrastructure in the form of roads and other public works would make the enlargement of the water supply network a very expensive business. Costs being so high, it would be hard for private companies to achieve profitability without raising prices beyond what poor people could afford. Privatization, then, is no panacea for water shortage in developing countries.

This objection does not hold, for several reasons. In the first place, 48 percent of the earth's population live in urban communities, and by 2030 this will have risen to 60 percent. Most of the additional 3 billion people born over the next 50 years will be urban dwellers, as will two-thirds of the people that need to be connected to a water network to reach the Millennium Development Goals.[98] William Finnegan, in a *New Yorker* article, puts it neatly:

> This enormous slow-motion public-health emergency is, in large measure, a result of rapid, chaotic urbanization in the nations of the Global South.[99]

Furthermore, UN-Habitat has shown that the seriousness of the problem in urban areas seems to have been underestimated, and that the lack of water and sanitation causes more serious harm in cities than in rural areas. For example, a water source a few hundred meters away from a household in an urban setting can mean hours of waiting in line, whereas in rural areas this can be a relatively convenient solution. Also, defecation in the open is obviously less hazardous where there is plenty of space.[100]

Last but not least, there are good examples of private investments with successful outcomes in rural areas too. One of these comes from Gabon, where in 1997 the government signed a contract with a French company to take over the distribution of both water and electricity nationwide.[101] The contract defined targets for the percentage of the population to be reached by the national grid and the water supply network and stipulated that prices were to be reduced by 17.25 percent. At the time of privatization the public utility was delivering water to 32 communities, but large parts of the countryside had neither electricity nor mains water.

The privatization has been a great success. In only five years, the company made 40 percent of the investment the contract stipulated for a period of 20 years. These investments have had the effect of raising water quality and lowering prices. The private distributor has also achieved all the network enlargement targets defined, and in some cases exceeded them. Fourteen percent more households than previously now have access to the water supply network.[102]

This only goes to show that poor rural dwellers are also an important market that commercial players cannot afford to ignore. In addition, the company has displayed such a degree of ingenuity that it is hard to believe a public utility could rival it. Among other things, as private operators have done in numerous cases, it has devised innovative methods for delivering water to households at very low cost.[103] The most convincing proof of how well water distribution is working today compared with its public-sector days is people's opinions. Customers, that is, the population of Gabon, are more satisfied with water distribution today than when it was operated as a public utility.

Casablanca

Centralization is one of the great problems besetting water supply in poor countries. Local players and representatives are far removed from power over water, which is wielded by politicians and bureaucrats in the capital cities, often in close collaboration with aid donors and producer interests. These, in turn, are remote from the users and have little incentive for making improvements. After all, they themselves are not directly affected. Decentralization of both the ownership and the administration of water can help to improve performance. Locally headed initiatives show that water can be used far more efficiently. We saw the positive effects of decentralized *ownership* in the Chilean example described earlier. But decentralized *power* can also yield positive results. The closer the decisionmakers are to the users, the more incentive they will have for improving distribution. Casablanca, Morocco, is a case in point.[104]

Demand for clean water in Morocco rose steeply at the beginning of the 1980s, partly because the urban population grew from 8.7 million in 1982 to 13.4 million in 1994. Meeting this added demand would call for investments—investments that the government, with its limited resources, had neither the capital nor the competence to make. So the government opted for a strategy comprising a number of measures. Two of them were the decentralization of power over water management and the admission of private interests. The cities, quite simply, were given a freer hand in deciding how to tackle the problem.

During the 1990s, a number of cities decided to invite private interests. Casablanca, the largest city in Morocco, formed a PPP that entered into force in 1997. A contract was signed with a private consortium consisting of a number of international and local players.

This private concern invested the equivalent of about $250 million between 1997 and 2002, inclusive. This, coupled with the firm's modern technology and management capacity, led to a whole string of improvements. Greater efficiency and reduced spillage enabled the company to supply growing numbers of customers with more water, even though it was producing less. The quality of the water improved. In addition, the company improved the management of effluent, even though this was not included in the contract.

The company has cut down on personnel strength. But on the other hand, more employees are undergoing further training today than when water distribution was a public operation, and personnel mobility within the enterprise is far higher than it used to be, with the result that more employees are landing in positions where both they and their employer are satisfied with their jobs. Wages have risen and are now decided more by the competence and performance of the individual employee. Health and safety conditions have improved, and an information technology system has been installed.

Furthermore, response to the users, who are treated like customers by the company, has improved immensely. Consumption is being metered more efficiently, distribution is far more dependable, complaints are fielded in a positive spirit, and faults are dealt with more quickly than they used to be. The local authorities, for their part, no longer have to devote a large proportion of public funds to water distribution but can instead make the social investments on which the cities of Morocco so strongly depend.

In a word, the private firm has contributed water distribution competence, experience of running a water company, capital, and technical competence. This was made possible by the decentralization of decisionmaking.

More Examples

Other examples can be quoted of water distribution in poor countries benefiting from decentralization. A study comparing water distribution in Senegal and the Ivory Coast arrived at the conclusion that, although conditions were similar in both countries, water distribution worked better in Senegal. Greater decentralization and local influence in that country can help to explain the difference.[105]

In addition to figures at the macro level and the cases we have now reviewed, there are a number of studies comparing water supply network coverage before and after privatization in various Third World cities. A trawl through a number of studies by the World Bank showed privatization to have increased people's access to water in all the cases investigated.[106] In addition to the cities and countries that have already been mentioned in this book, the review covered three cities in Colombia and one in Argentina as well as the increase resulting from privatization there. (See figure 7.3.)

Privatization and commercial involvement in water distribution also have a positive environmental impact. There are eloquent examples of public water-infrastructure ventures with very adverse environmental consequences. Political regulation of water pricing and supply has also had disastrous effects. In Pakistan, for example, low prices have led to overconsumption, causing sensitive mangrove swamps to disappear and biodiversity to diminish.[107]

It is common knowledge, from statistics and case studies alike, that privatization of public utilities generally has a favorable impact on the environment.[108] Private businesses bring with them new capital, new techniques, and management skills. Their pursuit of

Figure 7.3. Increase in water main connections following privatization in various cities. Percentages.

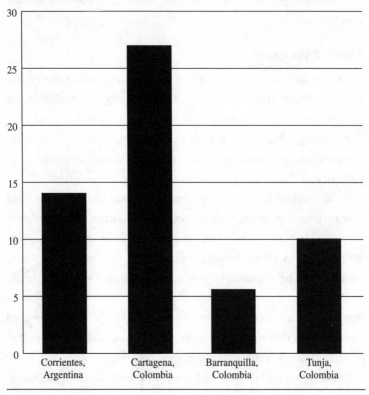

Source: Harris (2003).

competitiveness leads them to use resources efficiently. This includes the water sector.

There are two fundamental aspects to environmental problems connected with the world's water supply. We have to economize on our consumption of water, and we have to conserve the water available. The market and private enterprise make positive contributions to both components, in several ways.

Let us begin by looking at sparing use. Companies that live by distributing safe water to as many people as possible have a great interest in being as careful and economical with water as possible. They also have more competence and capital for effective resource management than public utilities, not least in poor countries. In Guinea, the private undertaking is more efficient and less wasteful of water than the public utility used to be.

We have also seen how prices determined by the market result in water being handled more carefully, and how consumption declines, as in Bogor in Indonesia. In Chile, the introduction of a water market has resulted in water ending up where it does the most good, which in turn has resulted in less water being used to create the same or increased prosperity.

As regards the protection of water as a natural resource, things are not looking good in the world today. For example, 20 percent of all freshwater fish species are endangered or have recently been exterminated. The worst situation of all prevails in the developing countries. In the Nile Delta, 30 out of 47 commercial fish species have been exterminated and a fishing industry that once employed a million people has been obliterated. On average in the developing countries, between 90 and 95 percent of all domestic wastewater and 75 percent of all industrial waste is discharged straight into the surface water, without any purification whatsoever. New Delhi discharges 200 million liters of raw sewage and 20 million liters of industrial effluent daily into the River Yamuna, which flows through the city on its way to the Ganges.[109]

Western companies, with the competence and capital to manage water and sanitation in keeping with quite different environmental stipulations from those generally prevailing in developing countries, will help to protect the Third World's water. Aguas Argentinas is a good example of this. This company's superior efficiency enabled it to reduce input of water purification chemicals compared with the situation when water distribution was publicly controlled. Commercial forces have made the company keep a closer watch on water quality, improve its water purification, reach more users, and extend the sewerage network in order to reduce the quantity of raw sewage discharged into the environment.[110]

Often it is the resources viewed as a common asset that fare worse from an environmental viewpoint. On the other hand, private owners will protect the water to the best of their ability. They make money by doing so, either by using the water themselves in agriculture or industry, or else by selling it. Formally recognized tradable water rights are the best arrangement of all. They have reduced the aggregate environmental impact. In arid regions, environmental impact is less in countries with recognized trading in water rights than in countries without such trading.[111] Formally recognized property rights also make it easier to control the management of water. If no one is responsible for water, there will be no one to regulate its use. Privatization has also induced governments to tighten up legislation and to keep a closer check on compliance with environmental laws and regulations. Of course, it is easier for a government to press charges against a private enterprise than to take itself to court for violations of its own environmental regulations. And having the threat of legal action hanging over one's shoulder is an important incentive for a supplier to follow regulations.

Privatization protesters usually argue that privatization will harm the environment, not help it. But it seems very hard for them to find evidence of this. Instead, they rely on anecdotes. For example, the Polaris Institute, in one of its pamphlets, mentions three examples of water companies being charged with violations of environmental regulations.[112] (Oddly, even though the focus of the document is poor people in the world, all three cases took place in Europe—not in developing countries.) True, mistakes are made by companies, individuals, and governments. We can always find examples of successes and failures, both private and public. That is the nature of human activity. The important thing, though, if we want to have a serious discussion about this issue, is the overall result at the global level. What tends to work, and what does not? And here, anti-privatization activists fail to present any evidence of private suppliers having a worse environmental record than public ones. In general they present neither data nor any analysis of the strengths and weaknesses of private distributors as opposed to public ones when it comes to the environment. Considering the record of public water suppliers, there are good reasons to believe that a full comparison would show the advantages of privatization.

Privatization of the world's water can have very good results, thanks to the superior availability of capital in business enterprise, the competence and efficiency of commercial undertakings and their access to technology, and also to companies operating for profit being motivated by quite different forces from those governing public authorities. Furthermore, the bidding process allows scope for competition among several enterprises. Private companies can also overcome efficiency-inhibiting deadlocks between different producer interests. In Cambodia we saw a comparison between public and private systems at one and the same point in time, and in Guinea a comparison over time. In both cases, the private régimes performed better than the public ones. In Gabon we saw that privatization can also produce good results in rural areas, and in Casablanca that good effects can be achieved through decentralization. Finally, we saw that commercialization and privatization of water can be good for the environment, as regards both reducing water use and preserving water as a natural resource.

But the admission of commercial interests to water supply is not wholly without complications, especially in poor countries, and we shall now turn to consider the risks that it may entail.

CHAPTER EIGHT

Hazards of Privatization

The role of the private sector in the ownership, management, and distribution of water is a very touchy issue, and one that has provoked a good deal of debate. To say that the question has aroused strong feelings, and that those involved in the debate have difficulty in reaching a consensus, is an understatement.

One example of this can be seen in the third World Water Forum, which took place in Japan in March 2003. Governmental representatives, international organizations, business representatives, NGOs, and others discussed a number of issues concerning the world's water, and the ministers taking part arrived at a joint declaration. This, however, did not address the issue of whether water should be owned, managed, and delivered under private or public auspices.

The issue was, however, addressed by those working at a lower level within the meeting. After lengthy discussions, they were still unable to reach a consensus. Their standpoints were simply too far apart. The statement summarizing the conclusions reached by the various working parties merely recorded that "[t]he debate concerning public–private partnerships has not been resolved."[113]

Why is privatization, or any opening up to private enterprise, such a delicate issue where water is concerned? Many other sectors, such as power, telecommunications, and postal services, have in various ways been opened up to competition and/or privatized all over the world, generally with highly positive results in terms of quality, productivity, and profitability.[114] The distribution of water, however, is considered different from other traditionally public activities, because access to water is literally a matter of life and death, even in the short term.

Although the point has been made several times earlier, it still bears repeating: There are very few instances of outright privatization of water, regarding both water as a natural resource and the distribution of drinking water. Instead, the most common arrangement of all is for water to be both owned and distributed by the public sector. In cases where private enterprise is involved, this is usually through concessionary agreements whereby a private concern rents the infrastructure from the public sector and undertakes to attend to maintenance and finance any investments, in return for being allowed to collect payment from the users. These contracts are generally long term, so that firms will be able to get a return on the capital invested, that is, make money. This has to be borne in mind when discussing the involvement of private enterprise in water distribution.

As we have already discussed, public sector–water régimes have a host of built-in shortcomings. Are the consequences of privatization so negative as to outweigh the weaknesses displayed by public water régimes? Let us consider the risks attendant to water privatization.

The most common point of criticism is that water prices will rise and the poor will then be unable to afford the water they need. But that question can be left aside, since we have discussed it already.

Another frequent point of criticism is that privatization of water means only the replacement of a public monopoly with a private one. One of the benefits of deregulation of public services and admission of private firms to them is that generally, competition is expected to exact better performance. But it is in sectors with natural monopolies that the benefit disappears, and instead a private company takes over without having to face competition.

Water distribution is a natural monopoly. An operator with access to a ready-made system of production, distribution, and purification has such a head start on newcomers to the market that real competition is virtually unattainable. Building up a new system from scratch is simply too expensive. Nor, from an economic point of view, is there any point in admitting competitors. One water supply network can supply the whole market with water less expensively than two or more rival players.[115]

Instead of a public monopoly, then, we get a private one that is equally exempt from competition and has no apparent incentives for behaving differently from the public monopoly. And private monopolies, unlike public ones, cannot be influenced through general elections. Companies are commercially, not politically, accountable to water users. In addition, they have a commercial interest in delivering water as cheaply as possible and at the same time maximizing their earnings. This, the critics maintain, is conducive to low quality and high prices. So the outcome, we are told, is that public monopolies are replaced with private ones that are very often still worse.

But do things really have to be this way? As we saw in the cases quoted above, there are private monopolies that function quite well. How can this be? There are several reasons, and they really touch on the causes explaining why private firms generally tend to succeed better than public ones.

In the first place, a private business can be regulated in just the same way as a public authority or utility, for those who believe public controls to be a good way of guaranteeing the distribution of safe water to as many users as possible. The contract between the public authority and the private distributor can be made to include rules concerning the price and quality of water, supply network coverage, and so on. This indeed is what actually happens.

In addition, we have seen both theory and practice indicating that a private company is more likely to meet such requirements than a public one, the reason being that private firms have greater competence and resources.

Furthermore, private monopolies are driven by quite different incentives from public monopolies. Imagine a water régime in which a private concern has a natural and actual monopoly of water distribution. The company is not subject to public controls of any kind regarding price, quality, or coverage.[116] A private, wholly unregulated distributor would, unlike a public monopoly, have an incentive for reaching as many users as possible. The enterprise lives on earnings exceeding overheads, and it would enlarge the water supply network insofar as earnings from the new users were expected to exceed the marginal cost of the work of laying water mains and the production and distribution of water to the new users.

Perhaps the most important point, though, is that the enterprise would have no incentives for using its monopoly status to raise prices excessively. True, we saw earlier that the price people are prepared to pay for water is quite high, but if the company were to raise the price excessively or if it started distributing water of unacceptably poor quality, demand would fall and so would the company's earnings. People would simply go elsewhere for their water, as is common, especially among the billion or more people who at present do not have access to piped water. Instead the company would find an equilibrium point for the price of its water, that is, a price level allowing a quality of water that as many people as possible are willing to pay for. The company would then achieve the highest possible income. The private monopoly would also have an incentive for keeping costs down as much as possible, enabling it to maintain the low water price. In addition, we should not forget that the companies have to compete for the contract during the bidding process.

However, a completely unregulated private monopoly may not be preferable to a regulated one. The price equilibrium might end up higher than a regulated price. How private water distributors are to be regulated, and how these regulations are to be enforced, will be discussed later.

Either way, the risk entailed by private monopolies and their negative effects can be taken as lower or slighter than the cost of people and businesses not having access to any piped water at all.

But anti-privatization activists also claim that the companies in the global water markets are so few that there is no real competition, that in fact they negotiate as an oligopoly, colluding to make profits on the precarious situation of the world's poor countries. [117] That allegation can be refuted in a number of ways. First, as the Polaris Institute, one of the anti-privatization NGOs, shows in a document, the number of international players in this market is not as small as many claim. In fact, the Institute lists, under the heading "Top Corporate Players in the World Water Industries," no fewer than nine multinational corporations involved in the provision of water in the world. That is no basis for an oligopoly.[118]

Second, the bidding procedures around the world for water contracts have been characterized by fierce competition. The major firms have been turning in very low bids (sometimes perhaps too low, as we shall see later). In the case of Manila, more than 50 companies were closely screened by the government.

Third, there are good reasons to believe that as the market develops, companies involved in related industries, such as construction and public works, will want to have their share of the market. By the same token, as water distributors are privatized in Europe and North America, some of them are likely to also head for the international market. As the Polaris Institute points out, "their [Vivendi's and Suez's] monopoly may soon be challenged by RWE, a German electricity and waste management company."[119]

Here, there is a clear contradiction among the members of the anti-privatization movement. When they want to show what an impressive and dangerous force the international water companies are, they focus on how many and how big they are. But when they want to point out the risk of oligopoly, they tend to emphasize how few they are. But you cannot have it both ways. There cannot be too many and too few players in the market at the same time.

So the main risks entailed by water privatization in the Third World are not prices denying poor people the water they are entitled to or private businesses abusing their monopoly status. Instead, the dangers entailed by admitting commercial entities mainly concern what happens in the actual transfer process— a bad contract, substandard procurement, political control, bad pricing, and so on.

But before going over these risks, let us consider a number of cases where privatization has not turned out so well, cases that have attracted a good deal of media coverage and debating attention. The best-known of them all is Cochabamba.

Cochabamba

Water distribution in Cochabamba, the third-largest city of Bolivia, was privatized at the end of the 1990s. Aguas del Tunari, a subsidiary of an American corporation, was granted a 40-year lease on water distribution. This is the anti-globalists' and anti-privatizationists' favorite example.

The water distributed by the public utility was heavily subsidized, which meant that its price fell considerably short of the true cost of distribution. AdT, however, charged a higher price, corresponding to its expenses. The price of water charged to poor people rose by 43 percent, while that charged to the middle class and commercial users rose by just under 60 percent. Demonstrations and riots followed, and people were killed and injured in clashes with the forces of law and order. In April 2000 the contract with AdT was repudiated, and water is now once more being managed and distributed under public auspices.

This case is usually highlighted to evidence the negative consequences of privatizing public goods. Almost triumphantly, various activist groups and NGOs have blazoned forth this unfortunate example as proof of the disastrous consequences of admitting commercial interests to the water sector in poor countries. At the same time, they have cynically welcomed disturbances in which people have been killed or injured.[120]

The contrast between a large American corporation's operation and the access of poor Latin Americans to water abounds, of course, in pedagogic simplicity and dramatic media potential, but news media reporting from Cochabamba have not conveyed an accurate picture of the true causes of the failure and disturbances.[121]

The first misapprehension concerns the price rises and the effect on ordinary people's finances. The higher prices are alleged to have compelled many people to spend as much as a quarter of their available income on water.[122] This is not the case. A 43 percent price rise meant the cost of water equaled 1.6 percent of an average household's income. For the poorest 5 percent of the population, the corresponding figure was 5.4 percent. Not even a doubling of the price of water would have resulted in any group on average having to spend as much as a quarter of its income on water.[123] Most experts argue that poor households are expected to be able to spend as much as 5 percent of their income on water. Assuming this is correct, the 5.4 percent cost can hardly be seen as excessive, nor can it be the sole cause of social uproar.

Another reason why people found their water bills higher than usual is that before privatization water was rationed, the reason being that the water mains were in such poor condition that leakages did not leave enough water to go around. These leaks diminished after privatization, with the result that rationing was no longer necessary, which in turn caused consumption to rise and billings with it. The unit price of water had not gone up all that much, but consumption had.

Another aspect to be factored in here concerns the workings of Cochabamba's water distribution before privatization. It was awful. For decades SEMAPA, the Bolivian public water utility, had failed to extend its network to the very poorest. Between 1989 and 1999, the proportion of households connected to the water supply network actually fell from 70 to 60 percent.[124] Those who were connected often had their supply cut off. Water was heavily subsidized, which mainly benefited the upper and middle classes, and it was these people who experienced the biggest price rises. The poor paid far more for water of dubious purity from trucks and handcarts.

UN-Habitat describes the inadequacy and inequality of Cochabamba's water distribution:

> Industrial, commercial and wealthier residential areas have the highest rates of connection, reaching 99 percent in Casco Viejo. Yet half of the homes in Cochabamba are located in the northern and southern suburbs, and in some districts in these areas, 1992 data indicate that less than 4 percent of these homes had potable water connection. . . . There is insufficient water provision to meet existing levels of demand.[125]

But the price rises are not the only thing to have been misrepresented. The blame to be pinned on the local authorities has been disregarded. The mayor of Cochabamba, Manfred Reyes Villa, known as Bonbon, had connections with companies that would profit from the construction of a dam, and he insisted, against the advice of the World Bank, that the dam be included in the project, which incurred an extra cost of millions of dollars.

Finnegan argues that some of the financial backers of the mayor "stood to profit fabulously from the Misicuni Dam's construction. When the central government first tried to lease Cochabamba's water system to foreign bidders, in 1997, and did not include Misicuni in the tender, Bonbon stopped it cold. It was only the inclusion of the project in the Aguas del Tunari contract that got the mayor on board."[126]

Another misapprehension has it that the political disturbances just came out of the blue. They did not. From the very outset, the position of Cochabamba's political leadership was weak and challenged. As Finnegan points out, "The dam project had less to do with how privatization works in theory than with the reality of how multinational corporations must come to terms with local politics."[127] The local political situation was a mess of patronage, populism, and vanity projects.

There are also murkier sides to the Cochabamba story. For one thing, the true victims of water privatization were powerful vested interests. Various groups that had previously been involved in the distribution of water (such as local water vendors and companies boring wells) felt threatened. Small farmers were tricked into believing, against their better judgment, that their traditional right to local water was threatened, even though a law had just been passed stipulating that this was not to happen. When SEMAPA officials could no longer be bribed to place wealthy households in a lower income class to qualify for a lower water rate, or when commercial customers could no longer be registered as households to the same end, suddenly these powerful groups found themselves with far higher water bills to pay. All these groups cynically exploited poor urban dwellers as an excuse for safeguarding their own interests.

It seems that the incidents in Cochabamba were part of a very complex story. Middle-class anarchist students, retired nostalgic unionized workers, forces with a vested interest in water remaining in public hands, and people who make up the large, informal economy of the city joined forces and used anti-capitalist and anti-foreign rhetoric against a primarily white government fearful of an uprising of the primarily Indian majority of the country.

Water distribution has been returned to SEMAPA. The poor of Cochabamba are still paying 10 times as much for their water as the rich, connected households and continue to indirectly subsidize the water consumption of more well-to-do sectors of the community. Water nowadays is available only four hours a day, and no new households have been connected to the supply network.[128]

Jorge Quiroga, then president of Bolivia, said, "The net effect is that we have a city today with no resolution to the water problem. In the end, it will be necessary to bring in private investment to develop the water."[129] The dispute between AdT and the Bolivian government has been brought to the World Bank's International Center for Settlement of Investment Disputes, where the case is still pending as of February 2005.

The Cochabamba case is much more complicated than it has been made out to be, and cannot reasonably form the basis of any conclusions as to the pros and cons of water privatization. If anything, it is an object lesson in how not to privatize and in the corruption, powerful vested interests, and populism that beset Bolivia and other parts of Latin America.

Buenos Aires

Another case of privatization that has attracted considerable attention comes from Buenos Aires, the capital of Argentina.[130] The background is as follows.

In 1993, the production and distribution of water were transferred to a private company, Aguas Argentinas. Up until then,

Buenos Aires' water distribution had been a sorry business. The public utility, OSN, had grossly neglected its infrastructure investments. Progressively fewer people were being supplied with water, the pressure in the pipes was steadily declining, and in summer the supply often dried up completely. Little more than half the 5.6 million people living in the poor districts of the city were connected to the water supply network, as against nearly all the 3 million living in the more affluent districts. Spillage was 45 percent, 99 percent of water consumption was not metered, and only 80 percent of bills were being paid.

Privatization changed things dramatically. Heavy investments and efficiency improvements radically boosted output. Potable water production in 1998 was 38 percent higher than it had been in 1992. The private distributor quickly reached a million more users than the public utility had, and within a few years the number of households connected had grown by no less than 3 million.[131] Thirty percent more households gained access to water pipes, 20 percent more to sanitation. The private company, then, was able to deliver far more water to citizens than the public utility had contrived to deliver. Most (85 percent) of the new customers were in the poor suburbs of Buenos Aires. They now gained access to water that was 10 times cheaper than the water they had previously been compelled to buy from small-time local vendors.

The price went down as well. In 1998, water cost 17 percent less than it had in 1992. Quality, which presented certain problems to begin with (mainly as a result of poor information concerning the state of the infrastructure under the public régime), was also appreciably higher in 1998 than it had been. Some of these improvements can be attributed to Aguas Argentinas raising money for investment and maintenance by actually collecting payment for the water. But the big change was the company's superior competence and capital, its greater efficiency, and its clearer incentives.

When the water authority was privatized, personnel strength was approximately halved, from 8,000 to 4,000 employees. OSN was heavily overstaffed and had four times more employees per water connection than the Santiago distributor in neighboring Chile. Absenteeism was very high. The average age of the staff was 50. Most of the manpower reduction, therefore, was achieved through retirements.[132] Meanwhile, all the investments entailed by the privatization project have created between 4,000 and 5,000 job opportunities altogether. The welfare effects of privatization—meaning its benefits to the national economy—were already estimated in 1996 at no less than $1.5 billion, $1.3 billion of which stayed in the country. This is a conservative estimate, because the figures do not include health improvements, a matter to which we shall be returning presently.[133]

Buenos Aires' water privatization was part of a whole package of structural reforms introduced in Argentina in the 1990s.[134] Thirty of the country's municipalities, comprising 60 percent of the national population, privatized their water distribution. Far more residents in municipalities with privatized water are now served by water mains than in municipalities that have not privatized. Not only have these privatizations led to people gaining better access to cheaper water of higher quality, they have also had important secondary effects, most important among them being a reduction in child mortality.

A large proportion of child deaths in Argentina, as in so many other developing countries, are from water-related causes, either water-borne diseases or lack of water for hygienic purposes. Diarrhea, septicemia, and gastrointestinal infections are closely connected with water. These three diseases are also included among the 10 common causes of death among children under five in Argentina. In municipalities that have privatized their water, between 5 and 7 percent fewer children are now dying from water-related causes, compared with municipalities where water is still supplied by public utilities. The effects were greater still in the poorest municipalities. Child mortality there dropped by a massive 24 percent. Water privatization in Argentina, in other words, has saved the lives of thousands of children, most of them poor.[135]

For all these good results, criticism of Buenos Aires' privatization has been unsparing. There is talk of greed, betrayal, and broken promises.[136] First of all, opponents point to allegations of corruption in connection with privatization, and rightly so: the politicians were far too closely involved in the process. But private players do not have a monopoly on corruption, which is also rife among public water utilities. (Enhanced transparency and the introduction of full cost recovery reduce the scope for corruption of privatized water utilities. How privatizations are to be carried out will be further discussed later on in this chapter.)

The "greed" argument hardly merits rebuttal. Pursuit of profit is the driving force of private enterprise. Anyone is free to have an opinion about profit, even to the point of calling it greed, but that is how the market economy is constructed, and so accusations of greed belong not so much to a discussion of water privatization as to the discussion of the market economy qua system, which is beside the point for present purposes. Suffice it to say that systems founded on "greed" have given citizens much better lives than systems without any such foundation. It is worth adding, and repeating, that profit is what impels companies to satisfy as many customers as possible, in the present case people who need water. And that is what the whole of this discussion is about.

The critics' main strategy, though, is to highlight individual cases, often of poor families who still have no piped water and no proper sanitation. These families are then invoked as proof of the failure of privatization. But the facts speak for themselves. The water is of better quality, 3 million more people are connected to the main supply network, and the price is lower than when distribution was publicly managed.

Another frequently cited consequence of privatization is that it often brings job cuts. Many opponents of privatization claim that prices will rise, but at the same time oppose any job cuts, which have the effect of reducing costs. They are against both these phenomena, regardless of their necessity. But you can't have it both ways. With fewer employees, the company has more scope for price cuts.[137]

The question, then, is whether staffing reductions are a good or a bad thing for an inefficient public operation. Does it make sense to refrain from privatizing an operation simply because the people employed by it then risk losing their jobs? If so, all the country's taxpayers and water users will have to subsidize a number of people who are in the wrong place. Poor attendance and low productivity show that many people were not all that happy in their work with the Buenos Aires water authority before privatization. The fact of the enterprise being able to produce more water than before with only half the previous personnel strength shows that it was greatly overstaffed. Applying the resources to something more productive is preferable to bolstering jobs in the water sector. The fact that at least a few of the staff of OSN seem to have been unnecessary employees gives further strength to this argument.

Furthermore, the workers who remained with the company seem to be better off than before. They own 10 percent of the company, and are better educated and better paid. The company uses better technology and has more computers and more professional management. Whether these improvements are less important than the layoffs is hard to say, but it is obvious that the issue is not as clear-cut as the union would have it.

But privatization in Buenos Aires has not been painless. The fact is that the price of water has gone up and down in quite an arbitrary fashion. Mostly it has gone up, but price reductions have happened. In 1994, when the first price increase occurred, many users indignantly refused to pay.

In 1997 the company wanted to renegotiate its contract, as did the public authority, in order to tighten stipulations concerning Aguas Argentinas' environmental performance. But the negotiations went badly, very much due to federal authorities dealing directly with AA, over the heads of ETOSS (the authority tasked with controlling AA). This resulted in prices to existing subscribers rising and those for new connections going down. Once again there was public discontent, with 51.9 percent of Buenos Aires' residents opposed to water privatization, as against only 38.6 percent in 1988.[138]

The need for new negotiations showed that the demands initially made were not realistic, and the company was also given to understand that it would come to little harm from not honoring its commitments.

In 1998 the price went up as contractually agreed, provoking something of a public outcry. The politicians on the ETOSS directorate were not able to agree on the prices that should be charged, because their different electoral followings had been unevenly affected by the price rises. The result was a highly fragmented debate, first between politicians and then in the press, causing discontent to spread to the general public even though water was still cheaper than it had been before privatization and many more people were now connected to the mains network.

In 2001 and 2002, Argentina went through the worst economic crisis in its history. When the government abolished the parity between the peso and the U.S. dollar, the peso nose-dived, and the government aimed to revise the regulatory and contractual framework applying to the privatized utilities. The company was no longer allowed to charge its customers pesos equivalent to value in dollars, since it would have tripled the prices. Aguas Argentinas thus saw its earnings—which were in pesos—fall dramatically in relation to its expenditures, which were largely in dollars. The company then wanted to raise the price of water to offset its exchange rate losses, but the national authorities would not agree to this. At the time of writing, February 2005, the company is still negotiating its contract with the authorities. An interim agreement is in place, but the Argentine government seems to be striving to gain full control over Aguas Argentinas, either by turning the company into a private-public partnership or by nationalizing it. Either way, it is clear that the government wants to define the rules of the company operations by itself.[139]

It is vital to observe here that there is nothing to suggest that a public distributor, which would also have been dependent on credits to make the huge investments needed, would have weathered Argentina's crisis any better. A public utility would have faced the same problem, and would also have been constrained to negotiate big credits to finance the investments needed for improving the distribution of water. The only difference would have been the utility being forced to seek compensation for rising costs through taxation instead of raising the price of water. The same people, then, would still have had to cover the costs, but less evidently so, because the fact would have been cloaked in a tax hike. Once again it should be recalled that the winners under public water régimes with general public subsidies are not the poor—neither those who lack mains water connections nor those who pay the tax that finances the subsidies.

The privatization of water distribution in Buenos Aires cannot be termed a failure. Millions more residents have gained access to safe water and need no longer make do with expensive water that is dirty and contaminated. On the other hand, the operation has not been a complete success. Why did it not succeed better? Analyzing the situation, Lorena Alcázar, Manuel A. Abdala, and Mary M. Shirley have explained that the privatization was flawed in three basic respects: asymmetric information, the wrong incentives, and poorly controlled institutions.[140] They already foresaw in 2000 that these faults would result in the privatization being called into question.

Let us begin with the information aspect. First of all, the bidding process was characterized by lack of information. It took place before the authorities had time to supplement or rectify deficiencies and erroneous information. These shortcomings concerned, for example, the quality of the public utility's infrastructure and finances. Some people in Argentina also claim that trade unions, which were opposed to privatization, destroyed records in order to make it more difficult for companies to evaluate the state of water distribution before bidding and, once in operation, to carry out the investments necessary to improve distribution.

In addition, Aguas Argentinas inherited an inefficient and impenetrable pricing system. Most users paid a fixed price based on the location, age, size, and type of their home, with any number of coefficients taken into account. This gave the enterprise a strong informational lead on both customers and authorities, enabling it to act opportunistically in relation to regulatory bodies and making it virtually impossible for customers to understand their water accounts and even more difficult to analyze price changes.

Moreover, ETOSS, the regulatory body, had a number of built-in weaknesses. It was supposed, among other things, to ensure that the company met its obligations under the concession contract and to impose fines if it failed to do so, as well as to receive, assess, and remedy customers' complaints. But the agency was newly formed and had to learn the job as it went along, added to which most of its staff were former employees of the public water utility, with neither legal nor commercial skills. The enterprise also had the advantage of ETOSS in terms of information. This, coupled with the contract enabling the agency to interfere in the details of AA's running of its business and make arbitrary stipulations, caused problems.

It was clear that the contract had made unrealistic demands from the outset. Aguas Argentinas therefore expected the terms to be amended. It was not alone in this, because the company that came second in the tendering process quoted only a marginally higher water price. As we were saying earlier, it is important for the enterprise to make money out of each new connection, so that it will be disposed to connect as many new users as possible. AA did in fact make money this way under the original contract, but the incentive diminished after the contract had been renegotiated and an extra environmental charge added to the cost of new connections.

The way in which the price was charged also created perverse incentives. Customers in expensive new buildings paid seven times more than other users consuming the same amount of water, and in this way subsidized their water consumption. Consequently, the company gained by first connecting high-income earners. Most users paid a fixed price. When the distribution network is enlarged, the marginal cost of connecting new customers will grow progressively higher, thus reducing the firm's incentive for connecting more households. In addition, with a fixed price, users had nothing to gain by saving water.

As regards the weakness of the regulatory body, we have already mentioned its disadvantage in terms of information. Its gravest weakness, though, concerned political interference. ETOSS was controlled by politicians at national, regional, and local levels. They in turn represented a variety of political party allegiances, and so

ETOSS was used for the pursuit of political advantages and its activities were frustrated by a good deal of political in-fighting. For example, the head of ETOSS was replaced far too frequently. To take another example, Aguas Argentinas was ordered to build infrastructure that was not provided for in the contract but that made possible a road construction project on which the mayor of Buenos Aires scored political brownie points. When the company wanted to raise the price of water to cover this extra expenditure, the mayor's representatives in ETOSS put pressure on that agency to sanction a price rise that probably was unnecessarily high. The fact is that the executive power (the president) interfered in relations between AA and ETOSS and supported the enterprise, thereby weakening ETOSS still further.

Despite these weaknesses, water distribution in Buenos Aires is appreciably better today than it was before privatization. Actually, when the author visited Buenos Aires in February 2004, not one person expressed the opinion that water distribution is worse in Argentina now than prior to privatization. And the people interviewed include many who, if they thought so, had good reasons to say that the situation is worse now than before, such as journalists critical of privatization; the financial director of the regulator, which at the moment is in a legal dispute with AA; and ordinary people in the street such as taxi drivers.

Why, then, has there been so much debate in Buenos Aires about AA and water distribution? There are several reasons. First, Argentina is in a state of post-shock, despite economic growth of more than 8 percent in 2003 and 7 percent in 2004. The economic crisis was very severe, making the country drastically poorer. A large chunk of the middle class has found itself poor. Unemployment is rife. This made the discussion about the price of water more relevant to more people. Second, the atmosphere in the country is filled with nationalism and anti-globalization sentiments.

The difference between the International Monetary Fund and Aguas Argentinas seems to blur, in many people's minds. After all, they are both expressions of "international capitalism and Western neo-colonialism," the forces allegedly behind Argentina's problems in the first place. And, as alluded to earlier, a foreign multinational is an obvious choice of scapegoat when politicians use blame games in order to cover up their own failures. It cannot be excluded that the nationalist and populist rhetoric that is rife in Argentina played an important role in the mobilization of privatization resistance in Buenos Aires. There are plenty of cheap political points to be made by pretending to work for the people and against a foreign multinational. In fact, this seems to be a common feature in the privatization debate. As William Finnegan, the *New Yorker* staff writer who broke the story about Cochabamba, mentioned earlier, notes, "the number of populists opposing water privatization seems to be effectively inexhaustible."[141]

Alexandre Brailowsky, head of Aguas Argentinas' special program to reach the very poorest parts of Buenos Aires, has a lot to say about the situation. He has worked with water distribution in different parts of the developing world for many years. With a background in Doctors Without Borders, he gives the impression of being a veteran from the Paris 1968 student uprising and is hardly a neoliberal ideologue or your average "heartless and greedy corporate leader." Therefore, it is especially interesting to experience the fervor with which Brailowsky rejects the claims and activities of anti-privatization NGOs in Europe and North America. He says that they know nothing about water distribution in the developing world and that they seem to have a very poor understanding of the real problems. In fact, he is quite upset with them. Other people in Buenos Aires argue along similar lines: "Perhaps you have efficient government in Sweden. In Argentina, we do not," people say.

Manila

A third instance of privatization noted for its negative conse-quences comes from Manila, the capital of the Philippines.[142] Before the private sector was admitted, only 67 percent of Manila's popula-tion were connected to the city water-supply network. Most of the poor residents were not connected, and instead were obliged to purchase bad water at high prices from local vendors who often charged 30 times the price of mains water. Millions of Manila residents, therefore, were spending as much on water as on rent. But poor coverage was not the only problem. Water, on average, was available for only 16 hours a day, and wastage was no less than 63 percent.

An NGO, usually very critical of privatization, tells us that "[l]ow pressure and illegal water siphoning caused contamination in the pipes, and waterborne diseases were common, increasingly through the early 1990s. In 1995, there were 480 cases of cholera in Manila, compared with 54 cases in 1991, according to the Philip-pines Department of Health. Reports of severe diarrhea-causing infections peaked in 1997 at 109,483—more than triple the 1990 number."[143]

Against this background, it is easy to understand that people in Manila were not at all happy with the public water distributor. It was chronically inefficient and had far too many employees. Public water, quite simply, was badly managed, even though credits had three times been awarded by the World Bank to put things right.

Water distribution was therefore privatized in 1997. The city was shared between two companies. Maynilad was awarded the contract for the western part, Manila Water for the eastern. The results were highly favorable. The companies quickly moved to expand service around the capital, and before long taps that had been mostly dry suddenly ran with cool water. The two companies raised the proportion of households with piped water by 23 and

14 percent respectively in only three years. By the beginning of 2003, nearly 10 million Manila residents were connected to the mains water supply, as against 7.3 million before privatization. Both companies improved their quality and their delivery performance. They used a number of new methods to reach the poor with their networks, after the innovative fashion characterizing business enterprises out to make money by their operations.[144] The new users could now get more water more reliably, at a fragment of the price they used to pay for the lower-quality water they had to rely on earlier. No more fights in the water line, no more spending long hours waiting in line to buy water from vendors who charged more than one-third of a family's income.

The public distributor could have made the same efforts as the private companies to reach the poor years ago, but it did not. The question we have to ask ourselves, then, is why? Notwithstanding the problems mentioned earlier, the question is of course very difficult to answer with any certainty. But it seems very likely that one or more of the following reasons contributed. The public distributor did not have access to or knowledge of the technology required. It did not have the incentives, and it simply did not come up with the idea because it didn't have the creativity that characterizes private enterprises.

But then came El Niño and drought, bringing a water shortage that was compounded by delays in a dam construction project managed by the public authorities. This was followed by the Asian financial crisis, and it became more and more difficult to connect poor residents to the water supply network. One of the companies, Maynilad, therefore asked to be allowed to raise the price of water, but the authorities refused to make such an unpopular decision.

The system now began to be criticized from an unexpected quarter. The poor protested and became more and more vociferous in their demands for price increases to give them access to cheaper water. Their argument was simple. If the price charged to those connected to the water supply system was raised by 5 Philippine pesos per month, this would generate enough capital for the companies to extend the water supply network to the poor residents of the city, who would then gain access to good-quality water at drastically lower prices. In this way, poor people without water would greatly improve their living standard. Oddly enough, no NGOs concerned themselves with this issue, nor did any other protagonists who usually sided with the poor. In the end, the government gave in to the protests and sanctioned the price rises.

But it then became increasingly clear to Maynilad that the consequences of the Asian financial crisis would be difficult to handle under the prevailing conditions. Maynilad, whose credits were in foreign currencies, was simply not earning enough to service its debts. On top of this, the company had assumed $800 million of the public utility's borrowing debt. Their contract contained a clause making it possible for prices to be raised in response to extraordinary exchange rate alterations, but this time the authorities dug their heels in. Manila Water, however, did not encounter the same problems.

Here, it is important to clarify some facts. The claim put forward by some anti-privatizationists that Maynilad has left Manila is not true. There were legal disputes about financial matters in courts at different levels, but these now seem to have been resolved. They got to write off some of their debt and were allowed to adjust the price to cover their costs. The main thing to remember is that despite what anti-privatization activists claim, Maynilad continues to provide Manila residents with water. And most important, millions of poor people still have access to clean and safe water at a much lower cost than before.

Intuitively, one might think that it is the company that should take the blame for the problems, and that is just what the critics say. But the question is whether the problem is not mainly a result of poor policy and of the circumstances attending the bidding, but that the companies had to compete for the concession by undercutting each other instead of tendering according to how far they could enlarge the water supply network. The focus of attention, consequently, was not on getting as many new users as possible but on curbing costs. Furthermore, the procurement was not transparent, nor was it based on any publicly stated governmental policy. It was carried through more like a panic measure, because the public water distribution service was so awful that the situation was becoming untenable. Consequently the population did not know what to expect.

Another weakness of this privatization was the stipulation in Philippine constitutional law that foreigners may not own more than 40 percent of Philippine utilities. The local firm behind Maynilad could not cope with the debts. But the French minority shareholder, with financial capacity of quite a different order, was prevented from stepping in because then the 40-percent ownership limit would have been exceeded. It was also clear that problems were posed by the authorities' refusal to allow the price increases necessary in order to cover costs, even though they knew, as shown in the argument earlier concerning Buenos Aires, that at the end of the day the cost would have to be borne by Manila's residents. Another weakness was the absence of an independent regulatory body to act as a neutral negotiator in the conflicts between the company and the authorities. As a result, the company was constantly having to negotiate with politicians who had difficulty justifying rises in the price of water. Last but not least, Maynilad had to take over 90 percent of the public utility's debts, which made it much more vulnerable than Manila Water to exchange rate fluctuations. If the debts had been shared more equally between the two companies, Maynilad would have had a better chance of weathering the crisis.

Here again, it merits repeating that despite the problems, more Manila residents now have access to safe water at reasonable prices than was the case before privatization. The Asian Development Bank describes the changes experienced by the poor:

> The number of poor households in Metro Manila connected to the water supply network has vastly increased. The households served now have access to better-quality water at a much-reduced cost per cubic meter. As a result, their consumption of water per capita has increased, their health is improved, and they have more time for other activities instead of having to quarrel for water.[145]

South Africa

One of the countries where the debate on private-sector involvement in water distribution has been most heated and most publicized is South Africa. In the introduction, we saw that former Water Affairs and Forestry Minister Kasrils took a very pragmatic attitude, arguing that without the private sector, the country will never be able to supply safe water to the 7 million South Africans who at present do not have a mains water connection. But the privatization process has run into heavy opposition, both from the country's own unions and internationally.

We shall not go into detail concerning South Africa's various privatizations, but there is a myth in the discussion that must be corrected. The opponents' most important argument is that commercialization will result in more and more people being unable to afford water, after which they usually refer to Kwazulu-Natal, where the worst cholera epidemic in South African history broke out a few years ago. The critics maintain that the infection was able to spread because the poor could not afford piped water and were forced to drink dirty water instead, while in fact the problem is that water distribution in the district hit by the epidemic was in public hands. So while the opponents' argument may have a bearing on discussions concerning price, and there is certainly cause to ensure that the very poorest can afford the water they need, as an argument in the discussion concerning privatization, the example of Kwazulu-Natal has no merit.

How Should Privatization Proceed?

True, there are cases where success has been limited. Most of the problems that were encountered, however, did not occur because of difficulties in reaching the poor with the networks (which, as we have seen, must be the single most important priority). Rather, popular discontent arose, often among the middle class and other groups with a strong political voice, against higher prices when public subsidies were redirected to other purposes. It should also be said that expectations among the public probably have been too high. But cases with only limited success are most often the result of bad privatizations, rather than of privatization as such. The two cases known to the author of this book where private operators have ceased their operations, Cochabamba and Tucuman (after the fall of Enron), are exceptions to the rule. UN-Habitat argues that these are generally viewed as isolated events.[146]

Since privatization has given millions of people, including many of the poor, access to water, we should not reject privatization per se. Instead we should learn from the mistakes made and pursue better privatizations. Hence, let us take a look at how a good privatization should be done.

As we have already seen, there are various degrees of private commercial-interest involvement in water distribution, ranging from simple service contracts, to a complete sell-off, to private interests of both water and infrastructure. Which model is really to be preferred? In order to discuss this, we should view the question from three perspectives. What does theory have to say, what does empirical evidence tell us (meaning: which model has worked best in practice?), and what is politically feasible? Given the positive effects that increased elements of market and enterprise are capable of achieving, and the risks entailed by public water distribution, it is appropriate to discuss two alternatives with as little public involvement as possible, namely completely privatized and deregulated water distribution and concessions.

Completely privatized and deregulated water distribution is very uncommon, but there are theoretical arguments in favor of it, not least when one considers the investment needs and the priority of reaching the unserved poor. In such a system, water may become appreciably more expensive to low-income earners who are already connected to the main supply network. The risk can be mitigated by the distribution of public water vouchers to the very poorest, as already discussed. However, the limitations of competition in this natural monopoly, with alternative water suppliers not being in a position to push main distributors hard enough to cut prices, may lead to higher prices than necessary. Furthermore, as argued above, a model this radical is probably politically impossible to implement, not least given the controversial nature of the issue.

Another possibility is a combination of water distribution concession and an entirely free market for water as a natural resource or "raw material." In this case, the role of the public sector is to rent out existing infrastructure and to regulate the private distributor. This is perhaps a more realistic solution, not least in view of the heated nature of the debate and the amount of opposition that exists. The fanatical, sometimes violent nature of the opposition naturally impedes commercialization and the involvement of business interests.

With this model, the enterprise still has a contractual obligation to a public authority, and not only to a collection of individual users. This is in fact the most common form of private involvement in water distribution. This model has shown good results in many of the cases we have been studying.

Using this model, one can derive benefit from the private firm's capital, competence, and efficiency regarding both infrastructure investment and maintenance and the actual business of distribution. And the company is financially responsible for these things. With free, or at least highly flexible, pricing, the company has a guarantee that earnings will exceed the cost of connecting new users and will thus have an incentive to reach as many households as possible. Perhaps the public sector should limit how far prices can rise before the contract needs to be renegotiated.

Concerning water as a raw material, a completely free market with tradable water rights will result in availability increasing, prices falling, and the water going where it does the most good. So, instead of arguing whether or not privatization can work, let us see how a concession of this kind is to be engineered.

One initial premise is that procurement must be open to as many tenderers as possible in order to guarantee the best possible competition, and the firms tendering must be able to compete on equal terms. All too often there are national interests or regulations involved that limit the efficiency of procurement. In Manila, for example, we saw how one company was forced to have a Philippine majority of shareholders, which made it harder for the company to obtain additional capital when it got into difficulties. And we saw how one company had done far less well than another, suggesting that there were better tenderers.

It is also important for the tendering process to be as transparent as possible. This provides less scope for bribery and other corruption and makes it harder for personal and other vested interests to influence the procurement. In the Cochabamba case, we saw what can happen when procurement is not transparent. The politicians deciding matters there seem to have been entirely devoid of fair-mindedness, impartiality, and common sense. That too, unfortunately, is pretty common.

Transparency and neutrality are also important when it comes to inspiring confidence in the process among both businesses and the general public. It is important not to try and score cheap political points, which was a problem in Buenos Aires. But transparency is also vital to the tendering companies so that they know what terms apply when they submit their tenders. Lack of transparency was an important factor in the Cochabamba failure and can account for the process proving less successful in Buenos Aires.

One obvious problem in many cases is that governments and public operators did not give a proper or complete picture of the state of the water infrastructure prior to privatization. This was usually due to the lack of complete records of the infrastructure. (In the case of Buenos Aires, there are even rumors that the trade unions destroyed the records in order to make it more difficult for the private company to take over.) Therefore the bids were based on false or incomplete information. Consequently, companies offered a lower bid than they otherwise would have, and once they became aware of the true state of the distribution network, they were forced to request price hikes to compensate for the investment and be able to meet their obligations. This, of course, made negotiations between the government or regulator and the private operator more difficult. It is thus important to make sure that the contract is based on correct and complete information.

Then again, we saw, both in Manila and in Buenos Aires, the negative effects that can ensue if the terms of the concession contract are unclear. This is what often happens when preparations are inadequate and the process is rushed through instead of being allowed to take the time it needs. Price changes had to be decided by the politicians, instead of the prices the company was allowed to charge being specified in the contract. In Manila this resulted in arbitrary behavior and also in a considerable delay in getting mains water to poor residents. Transition has to be allowed to take the time it needs, not least for careful formulation of the terms of the contract, but also to allow for public debate and consultation, a gradualist approach.

The terms, then, have to be as clear and simple as possible. This applies both to the tendering process and to the contract governing relations between the private distributor and the public authority. A contract must clearly indicate which risks and responsibilities are incurred by which player and the terms on which renegotiation will be possible. Vagueness in Buenos Aires created a breeding ground for political squabbling, corporate opportunism, and popular discontent. The relationship between the distributor, the regulator, and the government has to be legally based, not politically founded. The terms have to be open, distinct, stable, and based on rules. Combined with transparency and time, clarity could help us avoid repeating some of the mistakes that have been made.

Connected with this is the importance of depoliticizing the process, which is not allowing prestige or political point-scoring to influence matters. This applies both to procurement and to regulation of the water company. In Buenos Aires we saw the negative consequences of political interference in the form of arbitrary behavior and a lack of firm rules of conduct, which in turn had a string of negative consequences. One concludes that the process should be managed on a technical rather than a political level.

Another lesson to be learned from both Manila and Buenos Aires is that a completely new supervisory body should be set up, tasked with ensuring that water distribution is managed properly and that the company honors its contractual obligations. In Manila this role was allotted to the old water authority, which behaved more like an administrator of the contract than a regulatory body. Much the same happened in Buenos Aires, where the agency, moreover, was very badly equipped for its task. Given the apparent difficulty of putting in place an efficient regulatory authority in developing countries, there is much to be said for limiting its authority. This can be done by empowering it only to ensure that new users are connected, that pricing complies with current provisions, and that water distribution is of the quality stipulated by the contract. The authority must be strong, competent, and independent and its duties clearly defined and delimited. It should also be in place before the transition from public to private takes place.

There is a debate about the level of regulation private providers should have in a concession contract. There is a strong case for strong regulation, some would argue, since companies are apt to find ways to escape their obligations. However, it is important that regulation not hamper the creativity of enterprise to reach new customers. As we saw in Manila, this is particularly important regarding land title requirements and the servicing of poor neighborhoods. Therefore, the balance should be struck in such a way as to limit regulation, but to ensure the capacity of the regulator to enforce contractual obligations. There should also be clear dispute settlement mechanisms.

Furthermore, companies should compete, not by undercutting in price but in terms of how many new users they can reach. The most important matter, as we have seen, is not that water is too expensive, but that so many households do not have access to piped water. Therefore, the priority should be network extension, not price reduction. Governments should hire the company that can most quickly reach a given number of new households. The big problem in Manila was that the companies had quoted such low prices that afterward they were unable to connect any additional users, because no capital was then obtainable for the investments needed for enlarging the water supply network, as indeed was also the situation in Buenos Aires.

We have already discussed the negative consequences of under-pricing. But prices should not be raised dramatically. In Guinea, the price rise succeeded because transitional periods were provided. In Cochabamba, on the other hand, when prices were suddenly hiked they met with strong resistance.

As argued earlier, water distribution is a natural monopoly and water companies have little reason to fear competition from other major players. Despite this fact, concessionaires are often granted exclusive rights to serve customers in their service area. This is probably unwise. All residents are not reached by suppliers instantly after privatization, and they need to continue to be able to get their water from the usual sources. It is thus important to allow alternative provision of water to continue after privatization or at least in practice to not prevent alternative providers from operating.

One last point is that it is important to make sure that the terms and the operations are adapted to local conditions and that the company coming in has enough knowledge of these conditions.

Involvement of the private sector has demonstrably improved the water situation for millions of the poor and has improved the quality of both water and service. This is not to say that all privatizations have been smooth and flawless. There have been problems with transparency, corruption, and political and commercial opportunism in some company–government relations. The dividing line lies in how we react to these mistakes. Anti-privatization activists argue that, because of these risks, privatization per se should be denounced. I would argue that, despite its flaws, privatization has in general been beneficial, especially to the poor. Therefore, the neutral and logical conclusion, if you are driven by an urge to maximize human well-being around the world, must be to try to fix these flaws rather than to stop all privatizations. Any other conclusion that does not come up with an alternative solution is ideologically biased and does not take the perspective of the water-poor seriously.

CHAPTER NINE

The Poor Need Water, Not Ideology

Excessively low prices fixed by politicians have led to waste, lack of caution, and misallocation of resources—in short, inefficient use of water. Distribution, moreover, has been managed by bureaucrats and public authorities with a low level of competence, little capital, and distorted incentive structures. In addition, the lack of property rights and water trading has resulted in water being pent up in less productive activities, thereby compounding poverty.

In the developing countries where the private sector has been admitted to the water sector, more people have access to water than in the developing countries that do not have any private investments. Clearest of all are the examples we have reviewed, which show increased scope for the market and enterprise having very positive outcomes.

In the four Cambodian cities where water distribution has been taken over by business enterprises, the results are better than in cities with public water distribution. In Guinea, privatization increased the proportion of urban dwellers with access to safe water from 2 in 10 to 7 in 10, in little more than a decade. In Manila things went well to begin with, though problems arose when the price could not be adjusted in order to give poor people access to the water distribution system. In Buenos Aires, privatization, problems notwithstanding, resulted not only in more people gaining access to safe water at a lower price but also in a reduction of child mortality. In Chile, clearly defined and firmly maintained tradable water rights have turned shortage into abundance and resulted in nearly everyone today having access to safe water. In Gabon, we saw that private interests can do a great deal of good not only in the cities of developing countries but in rural communities as well. In Morocco, too, decentralization and privatization have yielded positive results.

Despite the evidence, there is plenty of resistance against the commodification of water. The water-as-a-human-right approach is much to be blamed for this.

Water as a "Human Right"

An international water conference in Dublin at the beginning of the 1990s laid down four principles.[147] One of them was that water has an economic value. Up until then, in most parts of the world, water had mainly been ascribed a social value, or else been viewed solely as a human right. In other words, it was felt that water should not be commodified.

The Dublin delegates argued that this perspective is inadequate. The status quo, with more than a billion people lacking water and millions dying every year, is unacceptable. More people than live in North America and Europe combined are without safe water, and a number of people exceeding Sweden's entire population die every year because of this deficiency. Millions of others are forced to spend most of their time fetching water. In this way, they are trapped in poverty. Billions of poor people in Third World cities have to spend a large part of their income on dirty, dangerous water because they do not have access to a water supply network. The Dublin Conference recognized that many of today's problems are due to governments the world over having overlooked the economic dimension of water.

However, putting an economic value on water has not been without complications. Strong reactions have occurred, and many parties to the discussion on water privatization maintain that we should go back to the pre-Dublin "water-as-a-human-right" approach. Water cannot be regarded as an ordinary product, such as soap or cars, it is argued. To sum up the argument: "Water is life. If we do not drink water, we die. Water is a human right and therefore it must be distributed democratically," that is, by the government. The UN emphasizes this approach, which seems to be growing in popularity in the anti-privatization movement.

This reasoning actually contains two parts: human rights and democracy. Both of these issues have of course been discussed at length elsewhere, but let us review the points briefly.

First, there is nothing undemocratic about letting a private entity play a role in providing what people need. On the contrary, there are plenty of democracies—even social democratic ones—where the private sector provides people what they need, such as health care. And of course, privately provided water is distributed democratically, since most of the countries that have commercialized water distribution are democracies, which implies that decisions to privatize have been taken democratically.

In contrast, keeping water distribution in the public sphere is often identified as more democratic. But it is unclear why that assumption is made. Using food as an analogy, we can observe that food is also essential to life. Yet in countries where food has been produced "democratically"—that is, by the government—there has often been neither sufficient food nor democracy. In this regard, water is no different.

Even if we accept water as a human right, that approach does not imply that water must be provided by the government. The International Covenant on Economic, Social and Cultural Rights does not rule out a central role for private enterprises.[148]

Again, the food analogy applies. Food is necessary for life, but nobody seriously argues that all food must be owned and distributed by the government. (Indeed, because food is considered a commodity, the world has been able to produce more of it and feed more people than at any time in history.) Likewise, there is no rights-based argument that justifies government management of water. The question that naturally comes to mind is why anti-privatization activists do not expend as much energy on accusing governments of violating the rights of the 1.1 billion people who do not have access to water as they do on trying to stop its commercialization.

Universal access to water as a human right has in fact long been promised by governments and bodies like the United Nations, without great success. It has simply been of no avail to have access to water declared a human right by innumerable official documents. Too many people still lack clean water, as has been the case for decades.

The 1980s was the official International Drinking Water and Sanitation decade, and as far back as 1977, representatives from most of the world's governments committed themselves to ensuring that everyone would have adequate water and sanitation by 1990. As we have seen, that was hardly the result. Political promises about public water delivery are not taken seriously. As UN-Habitat asks: "Why haven't the promises made by governments been met?"[149] To paraphrase one of the slogans of the anti-privatizationists, we cannot drink rights or paper, only water.

Against this background, it is interesting to read what Maude Barlow, a Canadian author of many anti-privatization publications and something of a star of the anti-privatizationists in the developed world, states in a document co-authored with Tony Clarke, director of the Polaris Institute. Discussing the case of Buenos Aires, the authors maintain that "Suez did expand water and sewage service by a small increment, but failed to meet its projected targets in both areas."[150]

Despite the failure to meet the targets, more people have access to clean and safe water now than before privatization (and, as indicated earlier, the expansion of service has not been as modest as implied by Barlow and Clarke). This must be a good thing. The question, then, is why Clarke and Barlow focus on failed targets rather than the expansion of service.

Anti-privatization activists use separate standards when judging public and private water management. As soon as any fault occurs in the private distribution of water, their anti-corporate bias, regrettably also to be found among more neutral commentators, persuades them to blame privatization in general. Similar conclusions are very seldom drawn in those cases where public water distribution does not work properly. Public-sector failure, in other words, is not attributed to the distribution being public, whereas when the private sector fails, privatization gets the blame.

In the debate on water privatization, the burden of proof is generally placed only on the advocates of private enterprise. Privatization is judged by the highest standards—often perfection itself—while public water distribution is subjected to no such standards. Given that approach, it is easy to see how any private-sector shortcomings would be judged failures. But in the real world, we must compare imperfect alternatives and determine which ones work best. In the comparison between private and public water distribution, the record shows that the private alternative has generally been far superior. Here again, critics of privatization fall short of providing convincing proposals to supply clean water to the billion-plus people who currently lack it.

One of the mega-stars of the anti-globalization movement is the Indian feminist and environmental activist Vandana Shiva. Author of the 2002 book *Water Wars—Privatization, Pollution, and Profit*,[151] Shiva has been a very active player in the anti-privatization movement. She seems disposed to blame all the world's water shortage on modern society in general and on the West in particular.

Shiva is hostile to development as such and blames industrialization for people not having access to safe water, which, as we saw earlier, is utter nonsense. She also ignores the fact that it is modernization, and the large-scale agriculture she so detests, that have made it possible to feed the earth's population and enabled humanity in recent centuries to dramatically improve its living conditions, not only in terms of commodity consumption but also with regard to "softer" factors such as average life expectancy, child mortality, and educational standards. A traditional lifestyle with small-scale agriculture would hardly be capable of providing 6 billion people with water, food, or any other necessities of life.

Shiva also highlights the spiritual value of water:

> A few years ago, a few thousand pilgrims used to walk from villages across north India to Hardwar and Gangotri to collect Ganges water for Shivratri, the birthday of the god Shiva. These pilgrims carrying kavads (yokes from two jars of holy water dangle and are never allowed to touch the ground) now number in the millions. . . . No market economy could make millions walk hundreds of kilometers in the muggy heat of August to bring the blessings of the sacred waters to their villages.[152]

True enough, no doubt, but it is extremely hard to understand how greater spirituality and long walks under severe privations would solve the world's water crisis.

GATS

Much of the criticism against the involvement of the private sector has lately targeted the General Agreement on Trade in Services, a trade liberalization agreement concluded within the World Trade Organization. Water is one of the services to which GATS refers. The affluent countries are alleged to be conspiring with their big corporations to compel poor countries to privatize their water distribution. There are even those who maintain that GATS "is designed to help transnational service corporations constrain and override democratic governance."[153]

That is utterly mistaken. GATS is an agreement on trade in services between countries, an agreement about liberalization. This means that a country that has an activity under private auspices and decides to open up that particular activity to competition may not prevent companies in other countries from competing with the native enterprise on equal terms. Sweden's Minister for Industry and Trade has put this very succinctly:

> I refuse to believe that poor people in developing countries benefit from private companies which sell services being spared competition.[154]

On the other hand, GATS contains nothing to compel any country to *transfer* water from public to private hands. So far, not one country has made any GATS pledge to open up its water market to competition from other countries. So much for compulsion.[155]

It should be clear to every reader that opponents of privatization appear to be united not by concern for the billion and more people without water, but instead by a general aversion to enterprise and the market economy. Their detestation of a system blinds them to reality and to the available solutions to the world's water shortage.

But there are more down-to-earth, pragmatic players who have realized that it is perfectly possible to believe in and promote both a social and an economic value for water. This has been admirably summarized by former South African Water Affairs and Forestry Minister Ronald Kasrils, who was quoted in the introduction to this book:

> In South Africa we treat water as both a social and an economic good. Once the social needs have been met, we manage water as an economic good, as is appropriate for a scarce natural resource. Some non-governmental organizations and international organized labor oppose what they call the "commodification" of water and

thus oppose cost recovery. We are concerned about this because absence of cost recovery leads to inadequate funding for infrastructure development and the resulting overuse leads to local shortages and service breakdowns which impact most heavily on the poor.[156]

The point of this book is not that all water distribution has to be private. Rather, the main argument is that an increased role for private enterprise and market reforms, if carried out properly and wisely, can save millions of lives and give water connections to hundreds of millions of people who today are deprived of it. It has been argued that there are well-functioning public distribution systems in the developing world, as in Porto Alegre, Brazil. But that does not mean that the privatization option must be rejected where the public sector has failed, as it has in most cases.

People who today are without water do not need dogmas and street demonstrations, they simply need water. Solutions are manifestly available, and it is thoroughly reprehensible that they should be disregarded for ideological reasons.

Notes

1. The story about Milagros Quirino and Fely Griarte is based on Asian Development Bank (2004).

2. CUPE.

3. See Spaulding.

4. See Spaulding; Public Citizen (2003a); Public Citizen (2003c); Public Services International (2000).

5. Kasrils (2002).

6. Saini.

7. Brook Cowen and Cowen, p. 1.

8. United Nations Human Settlements Program (hereafter UN-Habitat), p. 58; Hinrichsen, Robey, and Upadhyay, pp. 15-16; Holden and Thobani (1996), p. 4.

9. World Bank (2002); Woicke (2003).

10. Esrey, Potash, Roberts, and Shiff; Rahaman; United Nations (2002a) and World Health Organization; *Intersectoral Action for Health*, World Health Organization, Geneva, quoted in UN-Habitat, p. 62.

11. UN-Habitat, p 92.

12. United Nations (2002a), p. 18.

13. Hinrichsen, Robey, and Upadhyay, p. 17.

14. Sustainable Development Network.

15. ITT Industries, p. 1.

16. World Bank (2003), p. 2.

17. Ibid., p. 12.

18. See United Nations (2000) and United Nations (2002b).

19. The distinction between salt water and fresh water is not entirely relevant, for salt water evaporating from the sea and descending to earth as precipitation becomes fresh water. The quantity available for human use is a mere 0.007 percent of the total quantity of water in the world. Salt water is 97.5 percent and 1.75 percent is trapped in ice. Source: Wolf.

20. Lomborg, p. 134.

21. United Nations (2002a), pp. 8-9.

22. WDI Online; *The Economist*, p. 12.

23. Access to safe water is defined here as at least 20 liters of water per person

from an improved source, such as a water pipe in the home, a public standpipe, a protected well, or a source or rainwater collection point within a kilometer of the home. Regarding the OECD countries, these data are available for only Australia, Austria, Canada, Finland, the Netherlands, Norway, and South Korea, but there is reason to suppose that the proportion of the population having access to safe water is also very high in most of the other OECD countries. Developing countries are those with a per capita GDI of $9,025 or less (2001 prices). The World Bank classes these as countries with low or medium-low incomes. Least developed, by the UN definition, are the world's 49 poorest countries. Source: WDI Online.

24. UN-Habitat, pp. 120–122.

25. "Producing" water may sound odd, but water for distribution through water mains is treated in a variety of ways, including through filtration and chlorination. Water "production" refers to this process.

26. United Nations Environmental Programme and International Water Management Institute.

27. Asian Development Bank (2000), pp. 33–34. True, there are regions in these countries with a shortage of water, not least during certain seasons. But the fact remains that there is more water available for human use than is currently utilized.

28. ITT Industries, p. 2.

29. *The Economist*, p. 4.

30. Peter Gleick at the Pacific Institute, Oakland, California, in *The Economist*, p. 4.

31. World Water Council (2000), p. 1.

32. United Nations (2002a), p. 4.

33. International Development Research Center.

34. UN-Habitat, pp. xvii–xviii.

35. World Bank (2003), p. 2.

36. Winpenny, p. 2.

37. World Water Council (2000), p. 36.

38. Finnegan.

39. SIDA, p. 11.

40. World Health Organization, pp. 106–144; Moor, p. 78. Please note that the information on the Philippines dates from before privatization in Manila.

41. Asian Development Bank (2000), p. 43.

42. Moor.

43. Asian Development Bank (2000), p. 18.

44. Harding, pp. 1243–1248.

45. For example, should a riparian landowner be entitled to use all the water flowing past his property, without any consideration for those extracting water farther downstream? Another question concerns the partition of water rights in a lake between the riparian owners. And a third concerns the possibility, and desirability, of distinguishing between ownership of the land and ownership of the water connected with it.

46. Bate (2002b), p. 1.

47. The fact that I highlight the introduction of water rights in Chile in no way indicates support of a military dictatorship, as argued by some opponents. We must not close our eyes to policies that work, just because we do not agree with other parts of the policies pursued by the government in question. For example, it is difficult not to be impressed by the economic performance of China, even though the reforms are being carried out by a communist dictatorship.

48. Bate (2002a); Ohlsson, p. 18.

49. Holden and Thobani, p. 12.

50. Pakistan Water and Power Development Authority; Strosser.

51. Bate and Tren.

52. UN-Habitat, p. 104

53. Gleick.

54. Ibid.

55. United Nations (2002a), pp. 25-26.

56. Bate (2002c), p. 13.

57. Ibid.

58. Moor, p. 80.

59. Mohan Katarki, in Hinrichsen, Robey, and Upadhyay, p. 11.

60. Tren and Okonski (2003).

61. See, for example, Wolf, and Ohlsson.

62. Bayliss, Hall, and Lobina, p. 12.

63. MacCuish, p. 12.

64. "Full cost recovery" is the term for water bearing its own costs.

65. World Bank (1994); Moor, p. 83; SIDA, p 21.

66. Saini.

67. Lingle.

68. Kemper, p. 31.

69. Lomborg, pp. 35-36.

70. United Nations (2002a), p. 17.

71. *Water Industry News*; US Aid; "Water policies and agriculture."

72. Holden and Thobani, pp. 10-11.

73. UN-Habitat, pp. 61-72; Tynan, pp. 3-4.

74. Bate (2002c), p. 3.

75. Leipziger and Foster, p. 2.

76. United Nations Educational, Scientific, and Cultural Organization (a).

77. Whittington et al.

78. Bhatia, Cestti, and Winpenny.

79. Hinrichsen, Robey, and Upadhyay, p. 30.

80. Choe and Varley.

81. Moor, p. 86; Leipziger and Foster, p. 2; and Walker, Ordoñez, Serrano, and Halpern, pp. 8-10.

82. UN-Habitat, p. xvii.

83. *The Economist*, p. 13.

84. Gazmuri, p. 1.

85. Nickson (2002), p. 2.

86. The nomenclature of the involvement of the private sector is complicated and confusing with definitions typically not being widely accepted. A more appropriate term than privatization is perhaps *private sector participation* (PSP), which is the term used by the World Bank and others.

87. One possible objection to this argument is that private investments are made in countries that already have an infrastructure in place, because this makes it cheaper for the company to take over the distribution of water. The causal relation between access to water and private investments would then be the reverse of what is claimed here. This objection, however, can be dismissed on the grounds that access to water was measured in 2000 and investments were measured for the whole of the 1990s, which shows that it is private investments that have made the difference.

88. Private investments in water infrastructure 1990–2000, access to water in 2000.

89. These interest groupings could be called "ice triangles," a term analogous to the "iron triangle." The term usually denotes various constellations with interests in common, working together in the exercise of power, to acquire or retain privileges for themselves, often at the expense of other players and the general public. Originally it was applied to the so-called military-industrial complex in the United States, where debate, competition, and renewal were obstructed by the close partnership of industry, the defense bureaucracy, and Congress. Where Third World water distribution is concerned, it is tempting to dub the coalitions of interest ice triangles instead, but they have the same modus operandi as iron triangles, that is, strengthening vested interests to the detriment of the community at large.

90. Estache and Rossi.

91. This account of Cambodian privatization is based on Garn, Isham, and Kähkönen.

92. The following account of Guinean privatization is based on Utrikesdepartementet (2003a), pp. 313–328 (in the main report), and Ménard and Clarke.

93. Shirley.

94. Ménard and Clarke, p. 6.

95. Public–private partnership (PPP) is a term often used to denote different forms of cooperation between the public and private sectors, not infrequently on big infrastructure projects.

96. See, for example, Public Citizen (2003b), claiming that privatization leads among other things to inferior water quality, fewer people with access to water, and higher costs.

97. However, since the publication of the documents on which the account of Guinea is based, there have been further developments. Apparently, based on unconfirmed sources on the Internet, after the end of the 10-year contract, the

operator and the government could not agree on an extension of the contract. It is very difficult to obtain accurate up-to-date information on this case, but the situation seems to be that the government is in the process of finding a new private operator to run the water in Conakry.

98. United Nations (2002a), p. 15; United Nations Educational, Scientific, and Cultural Organization (b).

99. Finnegan.

100. UN-Habitat, pp. 48–50.

101. The following account of privatization in Gabon is based on the World Bank/PPIAF (2002a).

102. Harris (2003), p. 19.

103. Innovative methods to connect the poor at a low cost have been used by private operators in Manila and Buenos Aires (as we shall see later), as well as in Cartagena, Colombia, La Paz/El Alto, Bolivia, and South Africa.

104. The following account of privatization in Morocco is based on Nouha, Berradi, Dinia, and El Habti (2002).

105. World Bank/PPIAF (2002a), p. iv.

106. Harris, p. 19.

107. Sustainable Development Network, p. 1.

108. See, for example, Lovei and Gentry.

109. Hinrichsen, Robey, and Upadhyay, pp. 12–14.

110. Jaspersen, pp. 22–24; Lovei and Gentry, pp. 27–28.

111. Bate (2002c), p. 12.

112. Polaris Institute, p. 4.

113. World Water Council (2003), p. 2.

114. Galiani, Gertler, and Schargrodsky mention on page 1 a number of studies showing, in other sectors, privatization measures that have led to productivity increases. McKenzie and Mookherjee, quoting, on page 2, an empirical study of several privatizations with positive outcomes, maintain that economists tend to be in favor of privatization. In their report they also point to positive distributive effects of the privatization of water, electricity, gas, and telecommunications. Furthermore, Padco, on page 3, mentions a digest of 24 studies comparing the outcomes of private and public investments in infrastructure (infrastructure in general, not just water) during the past 30 years. Business enterprise performed far better in half the instances; in seven of them the differences were slight. The public sector performed better in only five of the cases.

115. Asian Development Bank (2000), p. 27. As we have already seen, there are cities with two or more water distributors, but these do not usually cover the same territory.

116. This discussion of entirely unregulated private monopolies is based on Brook Cowen and Cowen.

117. The NGO Corpwatch, for example, uses the heading "Busting the water cartel" in its campaign.

118. Polaris Institute, p. 4.

119. Ibid.

120. See, for example, Earthjustice; Kruse and Shultz; and Public Citizen (2003c).

121. The following review of the Cochabamba privatization is based, unless otherwise stated, on Nickson (2001).

122. See Finnegan.

123. McKenzie and Mookherjee, pp. 29-30.

124. Harris, p. 26.

125. UN-Habitat, p. 33.

126. Finnegan.

127. Ibid.

128. UN-Habitat, p. 26.

129. Finnegan.

130. Details given here concerning water privatization in Argentina are, unless otherwise indicated, based on Galiani, Gertler, and Schargrodsky; Jaspersen; Alcázar, Abdala, and Shirley; and Slattery.

131. *The Economist*, p. 7.

132. In Argentina, there is an expression, *Gnocchis*, for people who show up at work only on payday, which is the 29th of each month, the day that Argentineans traditionally eat gnocchi. Apparently, OSN had plenty of Gnocchis among its staff. They disappeared when Aguas Argentinas took over, which can explain a good portion of the layoffs.

133. Biche; Abdala; Alcázar, Abdala, and Shirley, p. 51.

134. The efficiency gains resulting from the privatization program as a whole are estimated to equal as much as 1 percent of GDP.

135. Galiani, Gertler, and Schargrodsky, p. 27.

136. This critique of privatization in Buenos Aires is based on ICIJ (2003a).

137. Of course, as mentioned earlier, public-servant trade unions have a legitimate interest in trying to save the jobs of their members. However, their interest does not necessarily, and often it does not, converge with that of the urban poor who lack access to water.

138. Alcázar, Abdala, and Shirley, p. 13.

139. In fact, Aguas Argentinas is under hard pressure from the populist president of the country, Nestor Kirchner, who, according to unconfirmed rumors, wants to hand over the water distribution to Spanish and American companies in exchange for favorable voting from these countries in the IMF on Argentina's foreign debt.

140. Alcázar, Abdala, and Shirley, p. 13.

141. Finnegan.

142. The above particulars concerning Manila come from Asian Development Bank Review (2003), pp. 6-7; Nickson, pp. 18-19; Slattery; Llorito and Marcon; and ICIJ.

143. ICIJ (2003b).

144. For example, they were allowed to disregard the stipulation of delivering only to households with formal title to the plot on which they resided, and the company laid pipes to which householders could make their own connections, using plastic pipes above ground, thereby achieving a substantial cost saving. (Nickson [2002], pp. 18–19.) A special pro-poor scheme uses small-diameter pipes to connect households to the water main and assigns maintenance responsibility to customers, in order to lower connection fees. Poor households were also allowed to pay for their connection fees in installments. (Asian Development Bank [2004], p. 52.)

145. Asian Development Bank (2004), p. 56.

146. UN-Habitat, p. 178.

147. Cf. "The Dublin statement."

148. United Nations High Commissioner for Human Rights.

149. UN-Habitat, p. xviii.

150. Barlow and Clarke (2004).

151. Shiva.

152. Ibid., p. 158.

153. Sinclair.

154. Utrikesdepartementet (2003b).

155. Then again, membership of the WTO is purely voluntary. Furthermore, every country, large or small, can veto any decision that affects it, and no country is in any way compelled by any other country to accept anything against its own wishes. This, it will be remembered, is not the case in the EU or the UN, an organization so often heralded by the same NGOs who attack the WTO.

156. Kasrils (2003).

References

Abdala, Manuel Angel. "Welfare effects of Buenos Aires' water and sewerage service privatization." *Anales de la XXXII Reunion Anual de la Asociación Argentina de Economia Polótica.* Buenos Aires: AAEP, 1997. <www.aaep.org.ar>

Alcázar, Lorena; Abdala, Manuel A.; and Shirley, Mary M. *The Buenos Aires Water Concession.* Washington, D.C.: World Bank, 2000 (Working paper 311).<http://econ.worldbank.org/docs/1065pdf>

Asian Development Bank (2004). *Bringing Water to the Poor: Selected ADB Case Studies.* Manila, Philippines: Asian Development Bank, 2004. <http://www.adb.org/Documents/Books/Water_for_All_Series/Water_to_the_Poor/Water_08.pdf>

Asian Development Bank (2003). "Water for all?" *ADB Review*, January/February 2003. <www.adb.org/Gender/review.asp>

Asian Development Bank (2000). *Developing Best Practices for Promoting Private Sector Investment in Infrastructure: Water Supply.* Manila, Philippines: Asian Development Bank, 2000. <www.adb.org/Documents/Books/Developing_Best_Practices/Water_Supply/default.asp>

Barlow, Maude, and Clarke, Tony (2000). *Blue Gold: The Fight to Stop the Corporate Theft of the World's Water.* New York: The New Press, 2000.

———— (2004). "The Battle for Water." *Yes Magazine*, Winter 2004. <http://www.yesmagazine.org/28water/barlow.htm>

Bate, Roger (2002a). "Let the market decide on water supply." *Mail & Guardian* (South Africa), March 1, 2001.

———— (2002b). "Pipe dreams for the poor." *Tech Central Station*, April 2002. <www.techcentralstation.com/030402D.html>

———— (2002c). "Water: Can property rights and markets replace conflicts?" in Julian Morris, ed., *Sustainable development: Promoting progress or perpetuating poverty?* London: Profile Books, August 2002.

Bate, Roger, and Tren, Richard. "Trading in water will lead to its efficient use and to its most equitable allocation." Johannesburg/Cape Town: Free Market Foundation, FMF (Article of the Week, Feb. 21, 2002). <http://www.freemarketfoundation.com/pmfull.asp?idv = 44&oid = 803>

Bayliss, Kate; Hall, David; and Lobina, Emanuele. "Water privatisation in Africa: Lessons from three case studies." London: School of Computing and Mathematical Sciences/Public Services International Research Unit (PSIRU), May 2001. <http://www.psiru.org/reportsindex.asp>

Bhatia, R.; Çestti, R.; and Winpenny, J. *Water conservation and reallocation: Best practice cases in improving economic efficiency and environmental quality.* Washington, D.C.: World Bank/ODI, 1995.

Biche, Alain. "Aguas Argentinas: A large-scale project." Presentation at the UN Commission on Sustainable Development (UNSCD), April 27, 1998. <www.wfeocomtech.org/UNCSD/AguasArgentinas.html>

Brook Cowen, Penelope, and Cowen, Tyler. "Deregulated private water supply: a policy option for developing countries." *Cato Journal,* vol. 18, no. 1 (Spring/Summer 1998).

Choe, KyeongAe, and Varley, Robert C. G. *Conservation and pricing: Does raising tariffs to an economic price for water make people worse off?* Paper presented at workshop on "Best management practice for water conservation," Hermanus, South Africa, September 7-10, 1997. Caterham, UK: Water Web Management Ltd, 2000. <www.thewaterpage.com/ppp_debate_8_varley.htm>

Christian Aid. "Ghana: Water: Trade justice campaign case study." London: Christian Aid, November 2002. <www.christian-aid.org.uk/campaign/trade/stories/ghana.3pdf>

CUPE. "Forum endangers future of world's water." Press release, Mar. 20, 2002. Ottawa: Canadian Union of Public Employees. <www.cupe.ca/mediaroom/news releases/showitem.asp?id = 87>

"The Dublin statement on water and sustainable development." *World Summit on Sustainable Development*, Johannesburg. Geneva: World Meteorological Organization (United Nations Hydrology and Water Resources Program), 2002. <www.wmo.ch/web/homs/documents/english/icwedece.html>

Earthjustice. "Urgent cases: water privatization." Oakland, Calif.: Earthjustice, 2002. <www.earthjustice.org/urgent/display.html?ID = 107>

The Economist. "A survey of water." Supplement to issue for July 19-25, 2003.

Esrey, S. A.; Potash, J. B.; Roberts, L.; and Shiff, C. "Effects of improved water supply and sanitation on ascariasis, diarrhoea, dracunculiasis, hookworm infection, schistosomiasis, and trachoma." *Bulletin of the World Health Organization*, vol. 69, no. 5 (1991).

Estache, Antonio, and Rossi, Martin A. "Comparing the performance of public and private water companies in Asia and Pacific region: What a stochastic cost frontier shows." Washington, D.C.: World Bank, 1999. <www.worldbank.org/html/dec/ Publications/Workpapers/wps2000series/wps2152./wps.2152.pdf>

Finnegan, William. "Letter from Bolivia: Leasing the rain." *New Yorker*, April 8, 2002.

Galiani, Sebastian; Gertler, Paul; and Schargrodsky, Ernesto. *Water for life: The impact of the privatization of water services on child mortality*. Stanford, Calif.: Stanford University/Center for Research on Economic Development and Policy Reform (Working paper 154), 2002. <credpr.stanford.edu/pdf/credpr154.pdf>

Garn, Mike; Isham, Jonathan; and Kähkönen, Satu. *Should we bet on private or public water utilities in Cambodia: Evidence on incentives and performance from seven provincial towns*. Washington, D.C.: The Public-Private Infrastructure Advisory Facility (PPIAF)/World Bank, 2000.

Gazmuri, Renato. "Privatization of water in Chile saves water, fights poverty." *2020 Vision/News & Views*. Washington, D.C.: International Food Policy Research Institute (IFPRI), April 1995. <www.ifpri.org/2020/newslet/nv_0495./nv_0495g.htm>

Gleick, Peter H. "Water Conflict Chronology—Introduction," August 2003. <http:// www.worldwater.org/conflictIntro.htm>. The chronology can be found at <http:// www.worldwater.org/conflict.htm>.

Gleick, Peter H.; Wolff, Gary; Chalecki, Elizabeth L.; and Reyes, Rachel. *The new economy of water: The risks and benefits of globalization and privatization of fresh water*. Oakland, Calif.: Pacific Institute, 2002. <www.environmentalcenter. com/articles/article1171/article1171.htm>

Harding, Garrett. "The Tragedy of the Commons." *Science*, vol. 162 (December 13, 1968).

Harris, Clive. *Private participation in infrastructure in developing countries: Trends, impacts, and policy lessons*. Washington, D.C.: World Bank (World Bank Working paper 5), 2003. <rru.worldbank.org/Documents/Private%20Participa-tion.pdf>

Hinrichsen, Don; Robey, Bryant; and Upadhyay, Ushuma D. *Solutions for a water-short world*. Baltimore, Md.: Johns Hopkins School of Public Health, Population Reports, vol. 26, no. 1 (September 1998). <www.infoforhealth.org/pr/ m14edsum.shtml>

Holden, Paul, and Thobani, Mateen. *Tradable water rights: A property rights approach to resolving water shortages and promoting investments*. Washington, D.C.: World Bank, 1996. <http://www.eri-la.org/Papers/water.html>

ICIJ (2003a). "Cholera and the age of the water barons." Study from the project *International Consortium of Investigative Journalists*. Washington, D.C.: The Center for Public Integrity, 2003. <www.icij.org/dtaweb/water/default.aspx?SECTION = ARTICLE&AID = 7>

ICIJ (2003b). *Loaves, fishes, and dirty dishes: Manila's privatized water can't handle the pressure.* International Consortium of Investigative Journalists, February 2003. <http://www.geocities.com/waterose_test/water03.html)>

International Development Research Center website, Ottawa, Canada: <www.idrc.ca/>; concerning water reserves, see <idrc.ca/reports/photoreps/slideshow.cfm?rep_id = .&pphot_id = 10>

International Water Management Institute, *Projected Water Scarcity in 2025* website. <http://www.iwmi.cgiar.org/home/wsmap.htm#A1>

ITT Industries. "Kenya," in *ITT Industries guidebook to global water issues*. White Plains, N.Y.: ITT Industries. <http://www.itt.com/waterbook/Kenya.asp>

Jaspersen, F. "Aguas Argentinas," in *The private sector and development: Five case studies*. Washington, D.C.: International Finance Corporation, 1997.

Kasrils, Ronnie (2002). "Ensuring the provision of water remains government's task." Article on the South African Government website, Oct. 9, 2002. <www-dwaf.pwv.gov.za/Communications/Articles/>

——— (2003). Address to African Investment Forum in Johannesburg, April 7–9, 2003, related in press release issued by the South African Government Department of Water Affairs and Forestry. <www.dwaf.gov.za/Communications/PressReleases/2003/SA%20View%20on%20opportunities%20for%20private%20involvement%20in%20Water%20in%20Africa.doc>

Kemper, Karin E. *The cost of free water: Water resources allocation and use in the Curu valley, Ceará, northeast Brazil*. Linköping: Universitetet/Tema (Linköping Studies in Arts and Science 137), Sweden, 1996.

Kruse, Tom, and Shultz, Jim. "Our response to the World Bank." E-mail letter to the World Bank, June 6, 2000, published at <www.globalexchange.org/campaigns/wbimf/Shultz.html>.

Leipziger, Danny, and Foster, Vivien. "Is privatization good for the poor?" *Impact*, March 2002. Washington, D.C.: International Finance Corporation. <www2.ifc.org/publications/pubs/impact/issue2/dl-vf/dl-vf.html>

Lingle, Christopher. "Coping water problems through privatization." *Korea Times*, June 14, 2001.

Llorito, David L., and Marcon, Meryl Mae S. "Maynilad: A model in water privatization springs leaks." Special Report in *Manila Times*, March 26, 2003. <www.manilatimes.net/others/special/2003/mar/26/200330326spe1.html>

Lomborg, Björn. *Världens verkliga tillstånd.* Stockholm: SNS, 1998.

Lovei, Magda, and Gentry, Bradford S. *The environmental implications of privatization: Lessons for developing countries.* Washington, D.C.: World Bank (World Bank Discussion paper 426), April 2002. <rru.worldbank.org/HTML/document_2028-html>

MacCuish, Derek. *Water, land and labour: The impacts of forced privatization in vulnerable communities.* Ottawa, Canada: The Halifax Initiative Coalition and The Social Justice Committee, read in October 2003. <www.s-j-c.net/Water_Land_Labour.pdf>

McKenzie, David, and Mookherjee, Dilip. *Distributive impact of privatization in Latin America: An overview of evidence from four countries.* Boston: Boston University/Department of Economics, October 2002. <www.bu.edu/econ/ied/seminars/pdf/mookherjeedpw11-7-02.pdf>

Ménard, Claude, and Clarke, George. *A Transitory Regime: Water Supply in Conakry, Guinea.* Washington, D.C.: Development Research Group, World Bank, 2000. <http://econ.worldbank.org/docs/1116.pdf>

Moor, André P. G. de. *Perverse incentives: Subsidies and sustainable development: Key issues and reform strategies.* Haag, Netherlands: Institute for Research on Public Expenditure/San José, Costa Rica, Earth Council, 1997. <www.ecouncil.ac.cr/rio/focus/report/english/subsidies/>

Nickson, Andrew (2001). "Cochabamba: Victory or fiasco?" *id21. insights*, no. 37, June 2001. London: UK Department for International Development (DIFD). <www.id21org/insights/insights37/insights-iss37-cochabamba.html>.

——— (2002). "The role of the non-State sector in urban water supply." Paper for *World Development Report 2003/04 Workshop.* Birmingham, England: University of Birmingham/International Development Department, 2002. <www.ids.ac.uk/ids/govern/pdfs/nicksonWDR.pdf>

Nouha, Hassan; Berradi, Mehdi; Dinia, Mohamed; and El Habti, Mustapha. "Drinking water distribution: The case of Morocco." Paper presented at *Water Demand Management Forum/Public-Private Partnerships*, Amman, October 2002. Ottawa: International Development and Research Centre, 2002. In French at <www.idrc.ca/waterdemand/docs/french/docs/Morocco_Original%20.doc>

Ohlsson, Leif. "Water scarcity and conflict." Paper presented at *New Faces Conference, Forschungsinstitut der Deutschen Gesellschaft für Auswärtige Politik, Bonn,* October 5-8, 1997. Göteborg, Sweden: Universitetet/Peace and development research. <www.padrigu.gu.se/ohlsson/files/Bonn97.pdf>

Padco. "A review of reports by private-sector-participation skeptics." Washington, D.C.: Planning and Development Collaboration International, 2002. <www.padcoinc.com/PSP%20Skeptics%20Report20Dec%2002%2012pdf>

Pakistan Water and Power Development Authority. *Trading of canal and tubewell water for irrigation purposes.* Lahore: P&I Publications 358, 1990.

Polaris Institute. "Global Water Grab: How corporations are planning to take control of local water services," 2003. Document on the web, scanned in March 2004. <www.polarisinstitute.org/pubs/pubs_pdfs/_gwgenglish.pdf>

Public Citizen (2003a). "Resisting the corporate tidal wave." Article on home page, scanned in October 2003. <www.citizen.org/cmep/water/conferences/articles.cfm?id=9355>

Public Citizen (2003b). "Top 10 reasons to oppose water privatization." Document on the web, scanned in October 2003. <www.citizen.org/documents/Top_10_(PDF).pdf>

Public Citizen (2003c). "Water privatization case study: Cochabamba, Bolivia." Document on the web, scanned in October 2003. <www.citizen.org/documents/Bolivia_(PDF).PDF>

Public Services International (2000). "Corruption charges dog water multinationals at world water forum." Press release, March 18, 2000. Brussels: PSI Brussels Liaison Office/Secretariat of the European Federation of Public Service Unions. <www.world-psi.org/psi.nsf/o/109af4ef31fdfe5cc12568b70033d243?OpenDocument>

Rahaman, M. M. "The Teknaf health impact study: Methods and results." Study presented at the international workshop *Measuring Health Impacts of Water and Sanitation Programs in Cox's Bazaar*, Bangladesh, November 21-25, 1983, in Moor.

Saini, Angela. "Scarce blue gold." *Frontline Magazine*, vol. 21, no. 3 (Jan. 31-February 13, 2004). <www.flonnet.com/fl2103/stories/20040213003103700.htm>

Shirley, Mary M., ed. *Thirsting for efficiency: The economics and politics of urban water system reform.* Oxford: Elsevier, 2002.

Shiva, Vandana. *Krig om vattnet: Plundring och profit.* Stockholm: Ordfront, 2003.

SIDA. *Management and use of water resources: A summary of SIDA's experiences and priorities.* Stockholm: SIDA, 1999. <www.sida.se/Sida/jsp/polopoly.jsp?d=1250&a=13754>

Sinclair, Scott. *How the World Trade Organisation's new "services" negotiations threaten democracy.* Ottawa: Canadian Centre for Policy Alternatives, 2000. <www.policyalternatives.ca/whatsnew/gatspr.html>

Slattery, Kathleen. "What went wrong: Lessons from Manila, Buenos Aires and Atlanta." Washington, D.C.: The Institute for Public-Private Partnerships (IP3), 2003. <www.ip3.org/publication2003_002.htm>

Spaulding, Holly Wren. "Busting the water cartel." Home page article, originally published in *Corpwatch*. Oakland, Calif.: Food First/Institute for Food and Development, March 27, 2003. <www.foodfirst.org/media/news/2003/watercartel.html>

Strosser, P. *Analyzing alternative policy instruments for the irrigation sector.* Wageningen, Netherlands: Landbouwuniversitet, 1997.

Sustainable Development Network. "Water for sustainable development: A sustainable development network briefing paper." London: Sustainable Development International, web document scanned in October 2003. <www.sdnetwork.net/briefing_papers/water_sanitation.pdf>

Tren, Richard, and Okonski, Kendra. "How to solve the water conflict." *Wall Street Journal Asia*, March 27, 2003.

Tynan, Nicola. "Private participation in infrastructure and the poor: Water and sanitation." Paper for the workshop *Infrastructure for Development: Private Solutions and the Poor*. London: Public-Private Infrastructural Advisory Facility, May–June 2000. <www.ppiaf.org/conference/sector.-paper2.pdf>

United Nations (2000). *Millennium declaration/Millennium summit, 6–8 September 2000*. New York: United Nations. <www.un.org/millennium/declaration/ares552e.htm>

United Nations (2002a). *Water for people, water for life: The United Nations world water development report*. Paris: UNESCO, 2002.

United Nations (2002b). *Report of the world summit on sustainable development, Johannesburg, South Africa, Aug. 26–Sept. 4, 2002*. New York: United Nations. <www.un.org/jsummit/html/documents/summit_docs/131302_wssd_report_reissued.pdf>

United Nations Educational, Scientific and Cultural Organization (UNESCO) (a), World Water Assessment Program website. <http://www.unesco.org/water/wwap/facts_figures/valuing_water.shtml>

United Nations Educational, Scientific and Cultural Organization (UNESCO) (b), World Water Assessment Program website. <http://www.unesco.org/water/wwap/facts_figures/basic_needs.shtml>

United Nations Environmental Programme (UNEP). "The world's freshwater supplies: Annual renewable supplies per capita per river basin." New York: United Nations, 1995. <www.unep.org/vitalwater/11-watavail-1995-2025.htm>

United Nations High Commissioner for Human Rights (UNHCHR). "International Covenant on Economic, Social and Cultural Rights," 1966. <http://www.unhchr.ch/html/menu3/b/a_cescr.htm>

United Nations Human Settlements Program (UN-Habitat). *Water and Sanitation in the World's Cities: Local Action for Global Goals*. London and Sterling, Va.: Earthscan, 2003.

US Aid. "Water-wise: A well of facts." Fact sheet in *Global Issues*, March 1999. Washington, D.C.: US Agency for International Development. <http://usinfo.state. gov/journals/itgic/0399./ijge/gj-07b.htm>

Utrikesdepartementet (2003a). *Mitigating risks for foreign investments in least developed countries.* Stockholm: Utrikesdepartementet (Study 2003:1). Summary at <www.utrikes.regeringen.se/inenglish/policy/devcoop/pdf/risk_study_executive_summary.pdf>.

Utrikesdepartementet (2003b). "Leif Pagrotsky tillbakavisar kritik om tjänstehandel-savtalet GATS." Press release issued by Utrikesdepartementet (the Swedish Ministry for Foreign Affairs), March 21, 2003. <www.regeringen.se/galactica/service=irnews/owner=sys/action=obj_show?c_obj_id=50034>

Walker, Ian; Ordoñez, Fidel; Serrano, Pedro; and Halpern, Jonathan. *Pricing, subsidies, and the poor: Demand for improved water services in Central America.* Washington, D.C.: World Bank, 2000. <http://netec.wustl.edu/WoPEc/soft/wopwobaiu2468.html>

Water Industry News, online journal published by Environmental Market Analysis (EMA Inc), New York. <www.waterindustry.org/frame-1.htm>

"Water policies and agriculture." Feature chapter in *The state of food and agriculture 1993*. Rome: Food and Agriculture Organization, 1993.

WDI online, *World Development Indicators*. Washington, D.C.: World Bank (2003). <www.worldbank.org/data/onlinedbs/onlinedbases.htm> (password required).

Whittington, D., et al. "A study of water vending and willingness to pay for water in Onitsha, Nigeria." *World Development*, vol. 19, 2-3 (1991), pp. 179-198.

Winpenny, James. *Financing Water for All*. World Panel on Financing Water Infrastructure, 2003. <www.gwpforum.org/gwp/library/FinPanRep.MainRep.pdf>

Woicke, Peter. "Making water work for development." *International Herald Tribune*, March 19, 2003.

Wolf, Aaron T. "Water availability: The politics of sharing." Paper presented at the conference *The Coming Crunch*. Baltimore, Md.: Johns Hopkins Bloomberg School of Public Health/Centre for a Livable Future, February 21, 2002. <www.jhsph.edu/Environment/Conferences_lectures/conference_archive/Population_feb02/Population_Feb02_Wolf.html>

World Bank (1994). *World development report 1994: Infrastructure for development.* New York: Oxford University Press, 1994.

World Bank (2002). "Water—the essence of life." Washington, D.C.: DevNews Media Center (Worldbank Group), May 17, 2002. <http://web.worldbank.org/WBSITE/EXTERNAL/NEWS/o,,contentMDK:20044610~menuPK:34457~pagePK:34370~piPK:34424~theSitePK:4607,00.html>

World Bank (2003). *Water—a priority for responsible growth and poverty reduction: An agenda for investment and policy change*. Washington, D.C.: World Bank (Working paper 25770), 2003. <www-wds.worldbank.org/servlet/WDS_IBank_Servlet?pcont=details&eid=000094946_03041604014623>

World Bank/PPIAF (2002a). *Emerging lessons in private provision of infrastructure services in rural areas: Water and electricity services in Gabon*. Washington, D.C.: World Bank, September 2002. <http://rru.worldbank.org/private_rural_infrastructure.asp>

World Bank/PPIAF (2002b). *Emerging lessons in private provision of infrastructure services in rural areas: Water services in Cote d'Ivoire and Senegal*. Washington, D.C.: World Bank, April 2002. <http://rru.worldbank.org/private_rural_infrastructure.asp>

World Health Organization (WHO). *Our planet, our health: Report of the WHO Commission on health and environment*. Geneva: World Health Organization, 1992.

World Water Council (2000). *A water secure world: Vision for water, life, and the environment*. Marseille: World Water Council (World water vision: commission report), 2000. <www.worldwatercouncil.org/Vision/Documents/Commission Report.pdf>

World Water Council (2003). "Preliminary forum statement of the third World Water Forum 2003." Marseille: World Water Council, 2003. <www.world.waterforum3.com/2003/eng/secretariat/0322-3.html>

Index

About the Author

Fredrik Segerfeldt is a communication strategist and senior adviser at the Confederation of Swedish Enterprise. Previously, he worked as an adviser for Central and Eastern Europe at the Union of Industrial and Employers' Confederations of Europe, a Brussels-based European business organization, and as an adviser for international affairs at the Swedish Employers' Confederation. Mr. Segerfeldt has been published widely in the Swedish news media and the international media, including the *Financial Times*, the *Wall Street Journal Europe*, *European Voice*, *Le Monde*, and *TechCentralStation*.

Cato Institute

Founded in 1977, the Cato Institute is a public policy research foundation dedicated to broadening the parameters of policy debate to allow consideration of more options that are consistent with the traditional American principles of limited government, individual liberty, and peace. To that end, the Institute strives to achieve greater involvement of the intelligent, concerned lay public in questions of policy and the proper role of government.

The Institute is named for *Cato's Letters,* libertarian pamphlets that were widely read in the American Colonies in the early 18th century and played a major role in laying the philosophical foundation for the American Revolution.

Despite the achievement of the nation's Founders, today virtually no aspect of life is free from government encroachment. A pervasive intolerance for individual rights is shown by government's arbitrary intrusions into private economic transactions and its disregard for civil liberties.

To counter that trend, the Cato Institute undertakes an extensive publications program that addresses the complete spectrum of policy issues. Books, monographs, and shorter studies are commissioned to examine the federal budget, Social Security, regulation, military spending, international trade, and myriad other issues. Major policy conferences are held throughout the year, from which papers are published thrice yearly in the *Cato Journal.* The Institute also publishes the quarterly magazine *Regulation*.

In order to maintain its independence, the Cato Institute accepts no government funding. Contributions are received from foundations, corporations, and individuals, and other revenue is generated from the sale of publications. The Institute is a nonprofit, tax-exempt, educational foundation under Section 501(c)3 of the Internal Revenue Code.

CATO INSTITUTE
1000 Massachusetts Ave., N.W.
Washington, D.C. 20001
www.cato.org